SUNFLOWERS AND SILVER BIRCH

Previously published work by Phoebe Hesketh:

Poetry

Poems (Sherratt & Hughes, Manchester, 1939)

Lean Forward, Spring! (Sidgwick and Jackson, London, 1948)

No Time for Cowards (Heinemann, London, 1952)

Out of the Dark (Heinemann, London, 1954)

Between Wheels and Stars (Heinemann, London, 1956)

The Buttercup Children (Hart-Davis, London, 1958)

Prayer for Sun (Hart-Davis, London, 1966)

A Song of Sunlight (Chatto & Windus, London, 1974)

Preparing to Leave (Enitharmon, London, 1977)

The Eighth Day (Enitharmon, London, 1980)

A Ring of Leaves (Hayloft Press, Birmingham, 1985)

Over the Brook (Taxus, Leicester, 1986)

Netting the Sun: New and Collected Poems
                        (Enitharmon, Petersfield, 1989)

Sundowner (Enitharmon, London, 1992)

The Leave Train New and Selected Poems
                        (Enitharmon, London, 1994)

A Box of Silver Birch (Enitharmon, London, 1997)

Prose

My Aunt Edith (Peter Davies, London, 1966)
    2nd edition   (Lancashire County Books, 1992)

Rivington: The story of a village (Peter Davies, London, 1972)
    2nd edition   (Country Book Club, Newton Abbott, 1974)

What Can the Matter Be? (United Writers, Penzance, 1985)

Rivington: Village of the Mountain Ash (Carnegie, Preston, 1990)

Sunflowers
and Silver Birch

A Memoir
by Phoebe Hesketh

Compiled & Edited by Catherine Robinson

UNITED WRITERS
Cornwall

UNITED WRITERS PUBLICATIONS LTD
Ailsa, Castle Gate, Penzance, Cornwall.
www.unitedwriters.co.uk

British Library Cataloguing in Publication Data:
A catalogue record for this book is
available from the British Library.

ISBN 9781852001841

Printed and bound in Great Britain by
United Writers Publications Ltd.,
Cornwall.

Acknowledgements

I would like to thank my family and my friends Robin Wineinger and Vicki Kestranek for their great support and contributions. Many thanks to my husband Derek for his patience, encouragement and technical skills.

I am truly grateful to all those who have made this book possible.

Catherine Robinson

Contents

Introduction
by Catherine Robinson

Phoebe Hesketh, my mother, was a force with which to be reckoned. Of all the people I have known and loved, she has had the most powerful influence in my life. I am Catherine, Phoebe's third child, to whom she gave the task of completing her life story. It has been an emotional journey and I have come to know my mother in a way that was not apparent to me during her life. I have laughed and cried out loud as she experienced the heights of joy and the depths of sadness. As to the content of the memoir, I have compiled her hand written drafts in a way that I believe she would have wanted. She requested that I include chapters from a previous publication.[1] I have also inserted photographs, poems from her books and personal anecdotes from her many boxes of letters and diaries.

Born in 1909, Phoebe was brought up in the north of England, and grew to love the moorland of Lancashire which became her home and final resting place. Despite their wild inhospitality, the rugged moors lay deep within

[1] *What Can the Matter Be?* published by United Writers, 1985.

her soul. Lines from the following poem *Northern Stone* are a testament to her passion for the northern countryside.[2]

> *Sap of the sullen moor is blood of my blood.*
> *A whaleback ridge and whiplash of the wind*
> *Stripping the branches in a rocking wood –*
> *All these are of my life stream, scoured and thinned.*
>
> *Yet breath of my breath, they have me by the throat,*
> *These dark, indifferent moors that take no care*
> *For life resurgent in the starving root*
> *And love undaunted by the hostile air.*

Two world wars passed during Phoebe's lifetime and although she was too young to feel the pain of the First World War, she describes the tragic events experienced by those around her. Her childhood and adolescence were deeply coloured by her father Arthur Rayner, Consultant Physician and Pioneer Radiologist, and her aunt Edith Rigby – a remarkable woman and leader in the Women's Suffrage movement in the North of England. She is the subject of one of Phoebe's later books.[3]

A firm believer in self-discipline, Phoebe lived frugally and sparingly. She and her sister Elaine were sent away to school at the ages of nine and six respectively. Phoebe learned to fight for herself and endure a bleak lifestyle which included sparse meals, lumpy porridge, ice cold baths, and strict rules. These conditions and the years away from home undoubtedly influenced her dedication to a regular daily routine.

She began to write poetry at the age of ten and developed a book of verse dedicated to her mother Gertrude Rayner. This poem comes from her handwritten collection:

[2] Extract from 'Northern Stone' in *No Time for Cowards* published by Heinemann, 1952.
[3] *My Aunt Edith* second publication, Lancashire County Books, 1992.

Winter

The red leaves of autumn
Have perished on the ground
The birds have flown to warmer lands
The flowers are sleeping sound.

The days are getting shorter
Sunny autumn's past,
The little rain clouds tell us
Winter's come at last.

She spreads her snowy mantle
Over all the town;
On the leafless trees
She lays her milk white gown

Winter in her beauty,
Oh! she is so fine
I think she nearly equals
The merry summer time.

Although Phoebe was scornful of her early poems, they illustrate her poetic ability and her love of the natural world. She considered her early small collection *Poems* to be unworthy of mention.[4]

Recognised for her academic talents, Phoebe's teachers encouraged her to apply for Oxford University. But as Phoebe often said, "the call of the wild was stronger than the call of learning." After completing her school exams in 1926 she returned home to her beloved countryside. By this time her mother had developed terminal cancer so her help was a godsend for her father.

Looking back in later years, Phoebe remarked: "It's just as

---

[4] *Poems* published by Sherratt and Hughes, 1939.

well I didn't go to Oxford. I might have become a dreadful blue stocking."[5] Indeed her creativity may well have been stifled by life in the academic world.

Some years after her mother's death in 1928, Phoebe met her future husband Aubrey Hesketh. She said, "he was handsome and smiling" and further, "I was determined to have him." They were married in 1931, after which she bore two boys. Martin was born in August 1932 followed by Richard in December 1935. She dearly loved her sons but became restless and in need of mental stimulation. The outbreak of war in 1939 together with long bleak winters led to her intense feelings of isolation. Aubrey, my father, as director of six cotton mills, worked long daytime hours. He also worked nights with the Home Guard as his wartime assignment.[6] Of necessity Phoebe was left to her own devices. Phoebe refers to my father as "a man in a thousand". He gave of himself entirely, always caring for the needs of others, rarely thinking of himself.

Happily during the 1940s, Phoebe met Frank Singleton who invited her to become Women's Page Editor of the *Bolton Evening News* local newspaper.[7] Despite misgivings about her abilities, she accepted the job. Frank was a hard taskmaster but thanks to his "scalding tongue and rare expressions of praise" Phoebe learned how to write. Her career blossomed and thereafter a succession of books was published. She also gave poetry readings, and lectured at local schools and colleges, to name only a few of her many activities.

Phoebe left the newspaper in 1945 and so began a new chapter in her life. After a reading to the Poetry Society in 1946 she met the poet Herbert Palmer.[8] Affectionately known as 'Tarka' because of his likeness to an otter,[9] he was a poet and

[5] Blue Stocking refers to intellectual frumpy women.
[6] Home Guard refers to Local Defence Volunteers operational 1940-44.
[7] Frank Singleton, Editor of the *Bolton Evening News*.
[8] Herbert E. Palmer, British poet and literary critic 1880-1961.

literary critic. Tarka introduced himself by saying, "You must be a reincarnation of Emily Bronte!" Recognising her talents, he became Phoebe's tutor and mentor and introduced her to many leading lights in the world of poetry. He made frequent visits to our home in Lancashire and with his help and guidance, Phoebe's first major book of poetry *Lean Forward Spring* was published in 1948.[10]

With regard to her poetry, the early poems reflect her passion for the countryside and the natural world. The nature of her writing changed following the death of her son Richard in 1948 at the age of twelve. This tragedy had a major impact on her poems which reflect her own fear of death and dying. Richard's death and my father's steady decline are reflected in the somewhat bleak nature of her later poetry. Lines from the following poem *A Boy Drowning* depict her personal suffering and her deepest fears.[11]

> *Drowning is pushing through*
> *a barrier like birth*
> *only the elements are exchanged:*
> *air for water.*
> *Then, water for air,*
> *my lungs*
> *folded flat as butterflies' wings*
> *struggled to expand*
> *in a round scream.*

Two years after this tragedy Phoebe gave birth to her third child Catherine and thus began another phase of motherhood. Often torn between the demands of family and her writing, Phoebe managed with the help of housekeepers and gardeners.

---

[9] *Tarka the Otter: His Joyful Water-Life and Death in the Country of the Two Rivers* – novel by Henry Williamson, published 1927.

[10] *Lean Forward Spring*, published by Sidgwick and Jackson, 1948.

[11] Extract from 'A Boy Drowning' in *Preparing to Leave,* published by Enitharmon, 1977.

One may wonder how she found the time and energy to write but everyday life events were a constant source of inspiration. Charming, witty, she had a host of friends, many of whom became the subjects and themes of her poems.

Phoebe had never allied herself to a particular movement or clique. Her poems are impossible to label, mixing humour with insight, using images from nature and everyday life to pinpoint her perceptions about life on this side of Eternity. Casting aside images of poets as romantics, she said, "Poets are realists; they go to the heart of the matter."

She did not strive for fame and fortune and tried her utmost to stay out of the public eye. Anne Stevenson commented that she was "one of England's strongest and most genuine poets." [12]

Phoebe's literary success is exemplified by the publication of sixteen books of poetry and four books of prose. Her poetry has been published in several literary journals such as *The Times Literary Supplement* and *New Statesman*. She undertook several radio broadcasts including the series *Prayer For the Day* which aired on BBC radio during the 1980s.

At the age of seventy Phoebe embarked upon the next chapter of her life. By this time I Catherine had married and moved to South West Ireland. Phoebe made regular trips to visit my family home. Phoebe writes: "I made at least twenty flights to visit Catherine and Derek in their bungalow in County Limerick." She fell in love with the magical country of 'myths and legends, pixies and fairies'.

After we moved from Ireland to the United States, she continued to visit and particularly enjoyed her trips to New England during which she made literary 'pilgrimages' to the homes of renowned authors and poets including Robert Frost, Emily Dickinson and Henry Longfellow. She 'met' her soul mates Henry David Thoreau and Ralph Waldo Emerson at the Sleepy Hollow Cemetery in Concord Massachusetts. About

---

[12] Anne Stevenson – British/American poet and writer, born 1933.

this visit she said, "Seldom have I left a graveyard with such a feeling of peace and uplift. Of all my excursions, I think that memory remains the most potent among so many that make me long to return to Massachusetts." In addition she gave poetry readings and a broadcast for a local television station.

Poet, writer, speaker, teacher, wife, mother, Phoebe's talents were endless. In her latter years she took up painting which she found to be therapeutic. Phoebe has been described as charming, contradictory, generous, straightforward and determined. Above all, she was my mother, my mentor and a source of comfort and guidance. As a child I put my trust in my parents and enjoyed a happy childhood with a stable, solid home. For this I am truly grateful. Phoebe relied on me during my father's illness and death, though over time, I felt the need to break away and follow my own path.

Phoebe's story will unfold in the pages that follow. Her childhood, adolescence, womanhood, marriage, widowhood are written in colourful vivid detail. The reader will discover how her life experiences and her beliefs have influenced her creativity.

Prestigious Award

In 1990 Phoebe was awarded an Honorary Fellowship by the University of Central Lancashire, formerly known as Lancashire Polytechnic. The following citation was read at the Awards Ceremony:[13]

"Chairman, Lancashire Polytechnic is an institution marked and distinguished by its distinctive character and mission. At the forefront of its distinguishing features are

[13] University of Central Lancashire Awards ceremony, December 1990. Reprinted with permission.

its commitment to the region which it serves and its support for the Arts. It is therefore doubly pleasurable for Lancashire Polytechnic to be able to honour a woman whose life and work have been centred on this region and who has made a major contribution, through her writing, to the artistic and cultural life of the North West.

"Phoebe Hesketh is a Prestonian by birth. She was educated at Birkdale and subsequently at Cheltenham Ladies' College. Her early professional career, like that of our other Honorary Fellows today, was in the media. She worked at the *Bolton Evening News* and between 1942 and 1945 she was the Editor of the Women's Page. Subsequently Phoebe became a scriptwriter and a freelance journalist for the BBC.

"Phoebe has also worked in education; she spent three years as a Lecturer at Bolton Women's College and subsequently spent several years as a tutor in creative writing in a number of Colleges of Further Education.

"Phoebe Hesketh is best known as a poet, and her first volume was published in 1948. She has been the winner of the prestigious Greenwood Prize for poetry on two occasions and she has contributed widely to journals and magazines. During the last forty-two years Phoebe Hesketh has had eleven volumes of poetry published, together with three books of prose. Her latest publication was published as recently as two months ago; entitled *Rivington: Village of the Mountain Ash* it is of particular local significance, describing Wigan, Whittle and Adlington and their surrounding areas in the nineteenth century. Always a prolific publisher, Phoebe has further poems due for publication in 1991.

"Phoebe Hesketh has a long and distinguished record of voluntary service. She worked for ten years with the Library for the Disabled and she served for five years as a visitor with Age Concern. Phoebe has always had a great love of the countryside and wildlife and for twenty years she was a member of the Executive Committee of the Lancashire Branch of the Council for the Protection of Rural England. Her particular interests today are reading and music.

"Chairman, it is gratifying for Lancashire Polytechnic to be able to honour a woman whose professional and voluntary work has done so much to contribute to the cultural richness of the region where we are centred. It is an honour and pleasure to present to you, for the award of an Honorary Fellowship of Lancashire Polytechnic, Phoebe Hesketh."

Chapter 1

Early Years

The room was filled with sunlight, and in a golden cage a canary was singing. That first glimpse of spring with curtains, paint, and ottoman of apple-green, is all I remember of the day-nursery. I was born in January 1909, therefore this must have been somewhere in the spring of the following year. I've always had a good memory. For instance, I remember lying in my wooden drop-side cot while someone in a white cap and apron sang "Oh dear, what can the matter be?" Apt words for the early days of a doctor's daughter. I remember, also, throwing toys from a maroon pram on to the pavement outside Number One Ribblesdale Place, Preston.

Another clear memory is of a March day in 1912 spitting with rain. I was wearing a beige woollen jacket and cap as I walked with my mother along the street to Number Nine, Ribblesdale Place which for the next ten years, was to be my home. Number Nine had a two-tiered garden bordered by a wall topped with broken glass, that looked south over Avenham Park to the broad curving bend of the Ribble. I loved the river and the bridge with its many arches over which roared the expresses from London on their way to Glasgow. This was the line of the London North Western Railway whose trains at night became dragons spitting fire; their sparks illuminated the ostrich plumes of smoke curling over the tops of the following carriages. These trains, to me, became lullabies sending me to sleep in deep and distant lands. This was while I lay in a canopied double bed, divided by a bolster from my sister Elaine, born on July 2nd after our arrival in the new house.

Thereafter, from the age of three, memories crowd in, jumbled in time, but mostly of sunny summer days. There were daily walks in the park with nannies, except on their longed-for days off when Mother took charge of us and made our outings interesting with her talk and observations. These walks also took place after Sunday matins at the parish church of which I remember nothing but the gossamer-thin flags hanging from the roof, and the interminable droning through three psalms.

This church ritual accomplished, it seemed that all the 'Quality' from the posh neighbourhoods of Ribblesdale Place and Winckley Square paraded in Miller Park; that is, all the ladies of professional men: wives, sisters and daughters of lawyers, doctors and dentists, but not schoolmasters whom Jane Austen had considered a cut below. I remember the brightly-coloured silks and satins of long dresses, the ostrich plumes and parasols, and the wide-brimmed hats, feathered or flowered. If sleeves were short, long gloves were worn. On one occasion, in the middle of the parade, we stopped in front of the statue of Lord Derby, bespattered with tar since 1913. "Your Aunt Edith did that,"[14] my mother said, tight-lipped with disapproval, but never in front of her friends, all of whom shied away from the militant suffragettes. Indeed, my mother was acutely embarrassed by the notoriety of her sister-in-law who lived round the corner in Winckley Square, the wife of a

[14] Edith Rigby – British suffragette, 1872-1948.

loved and respected doctor, Charles Rigby, affectionately known to us as 'Uncle Charlie'.

Wearing long, homespun sack-like gowns and sandals, Edith would never have dreamed of parading in Miller Park below the statue who's tarring she had, in fact, arranged, but not carried out. At that moment she was in Walton Gaol on hunger strike, being forcibly fed not for this but for a more dastardly outrage. On July 7th she had, unaided and alone, poured a paraffin trail around Lord Leverhulme's bungalow on Rivington Pike.[15] After lighting it she hurried downhill to be speeded away in her husband's Humber Snipe which awaited her, with chauffeur, at the Black Horse pub. The blaze from the fire, now well alight, was seen by the astonished villagers, and raged on until the following midday.

Sometimes I heard my Aunt Edith alluded to in shocked undertones by the ladies in the park whose main occupations seemed to be giving dinner and bridge parties. After this midday ritual, we returned gleefully home to roast beef, Yorkshire pudding and apple pie. We always waited till half-past one for this feast. My father seldom finished his Sunday rounds till long after two by which time Mother would tell a fretting cook to serve up. Only on Sundays were we children allowed lunch in the dining room which turned out to be a mixed blessing with Mother trying to appease cook and staunch Father's irritation at overdone beef.

By now it's obvious that he was a doctor in general practice though at the time he was fitting up a room with X-ray apparatus, a science-fiction monster generating humming noises and crackles while emitting blue sparks. No need to forbid entry to Elaine and me; we cowered away in terror. This was probably one of the first private X-ray machines to be installed in Great Britain. And since 1904 he had directed the first hospital X-ray department in the country, at the Preston

[15] Lord Leverhulme: William Hesketh Lever, industrialist/politician, 1851-1925.

Royal Infirmary known to our Roman Catholic cook as the R.I.P.

Later generations have deplored the treatment of domestic servants at this time; a term my mother would never allow, we called them maids. All the same I know ours were well fed and housed by comparison to the factory and shop girls. Factory girls, at this time, had to work twelve or fourteen hour days for scant wages. At the turn of the century a beginner in the weaving mills, known as a half-timer from the age of eleven, worked at least six hours for two and nine pence a week. Full-timers, at eighteen, received five and six pence a week.

It was against these conditions that Edith went to war. The story of her campaigns for women's rights has been told elsewhere.[16] Neighbours critical of her often failed to realise that she was also championing their rights and seemed content to regard men as superior beings. Though they often drew veils over their husbands' misdoings, an erring wife was generally shut out from their society.

One morning there was an uproar in Winckley Square when Edith appeared on her front doorsteps wearing an apron. Beside her was the freckled, red-haired boy she'd adopted from the Harris Orphanage. Together they knelt down and scrubbed the steps, "Bringing disgrace to the whole neighbourhood," exclaimed a haughty lady speaking for all. Indignation grew when she was seen in the Square gardens rolling this same boy in the dust. "Just like the sparrows," she explained; "They love having dust baths. Too many of us humans have broken away from our natural roots."

Eventually a deputation knocked on her door demanding that she leave the neighbourhood, the tone of which she was lowering. Next morning the door of their leader was mysteriously coated in whitewash.

My mother never set foot in Aunt Edith's house, but I, Uncle

[16] *My Aunt Edith*, second publication, Lancashire County Books, 1992.

21

Charlie's god-daughter, was sometimes sent there for tea with my nanny who dropped me on the doorstep. But I don't ever remember having tea. Either her housekeeper was having the afternoon off, or I was too intrigued by my aunt's talk to remember. Instead of tea she talked to me in her low, gentle voice, entrancing me with stories of Brer Rabbit and Brer Fox, and a sheepdog called Rab. She had laughing blue eyes and bobbed hair – an ultra new fashion from America deplored by the neighbours. As I've already said, she wore homespun and sandals, and a heavy chain set with large coloured stones around her neck. Whatever her goings-on outside, she was the quietest, most gentle person I've ever met, and belonged to another world from my pretty mother who was always so well and becomingly dressed.

I entered another world in our kitchen ruled over by Kate, the Irish cook in whose reign a succession of house-parlour maids came and went. Here I watched knives brightened and sharpened in a machine which ground round and round like a wheel, flat irons laid on red-hot coals, and heated goffering irons curling rows of frills on our petticoats and knickers. Much gossip and laughter enlivened kitchen tea, hot and strong with bread, butter, jam and seed cake. From the window we watched the horse-drawn delivery vans, the coal-man emptying sacks of coal down a hole in the pavement outside, and in the mornings the milkman measuring pints from huge metal cans. Then there was the rag-and-bone man with his ribby pony shouting for contributions from his rickety two-wheeled cart. Best of all, I remember a funeral from the opposite house where a hearse drew up behind four massive black horses with feathered fetlocks, and plumes in black and purple waving on their heads. All was black, including the front door draped in black velvet, the undertakers with black ribbons in their hats, and the mourners who climbed, black-clad, into the following carriages each drawn by two black horses, or one according to relationship with the deceased. Kate at this point crossed herself and murmured "R.I.P".

To leave the house for the garden, in which the lower lawn prided itself on a white cherry tree. There was also a dark brown summerhouse, loosely thatched, and curtained with spiders' webs. A dim light struggled luridly through tiny coloured glass windows. We avoided this sinister hiding-place except when chased by two horrid boys who lived across the road. Elaine, only four years old at the time, was regarded as 'uninteresting', but I was closely inspected, petticoats up, knickers down with all their frills on the floor. Bewildered, I was unresistant, bored, and quite unimpressed by the solitary limp object produced from their trousers. But when ordered to 'lick it' I drew back.

I loved my lessons at Preston High School which stood solid and gracious in red Georgian brick on the top side of Winckley Square. I can vividly remember my first lessons in history. I see King Harold on a high hill of sand, looking upward when an arrow shot by one of William's men pierced him in the eye and killed him. The Army of Conquest sailed over the Channel to invade us, as the Romans had done before. Here and there were sown the seeds of pride in our island race – seeds which grew and multiplied, and are now about to be scattered. I can see the oak root over which the horse of William Rufus was destined to stumble and bring the rider to his death.

Reading by pictorial alphabet, writing with pot-hooks; spelling and learning by heart and by rule was a soothing and reassuring exercise. We added and subtracted with coloured beads before reaching the more difficult fractions by several heaps of butter beans. This was the order in 1914.

After the outbreak of war in August, my father enlisted in the army and early in 1915, he was commissioned as an officer in the Royal Army Medical Corps (RAMC) and drafted to the

Middle East for over four years. Meanwhile my mother worked for the Red Cross and three nights a week she served all night in the buffet on Preston station where 'men in blue' home on leave thronged for tea and sandwiches. War work on the home front was inevitably drab and lonely. Both our parents had become rather shadowy figures so we children were left largely to our own devices. Our idle summers were divided by wartime winters and childhood ailments.

In December 1915 I woke one morning to a fierce rash on my chest which turned out to be measles. A week later, my sister Elaine contracted whooping cough. We were both made ill by swapping each other's diseases which, without the help of prophylactics, were dire complaints in those days. Then my poor mother fell victim to whooping cough. Bedfast in the same room, we were sick together and in turns, by day and by night for weeks on end.

By March 1916 we were all three woefully reduced. My weight on the consulting room scales caused concern and the doctor ordered cod liver oil with malt and iron tablets to supplement a wartime diet lacking in butter, eggs, fruit and vegetables. I must have been in a very poor way physically, for my mother to consent to sending me to stay with Aunt Edith in the country.

My aunt had emerged from the suffragette movement to choose the peaceful green of work on the land for her war effort. For this purpose she took Marigold Cottage which, complete with thatch, washed to the colour of its name, stood between high hedges three miles west of Preston. Two acres of well-planted garden led to an orchard and a row of six white beehives. So began an era which replaced strife with harmony in the universe. My aunt, new-born in breeches and haymakers smock, greeted me on this visit of recovery from a series of illnesses. This restorative visit was the first of many during the summer and autumn of 1915 with my sister Elaine. After seven prison sentences Aunt Edith appeared as a gaunt figure, short grey hair wispy in the wind. Her movements, whether swinging buckets, wheeling barrows, or digging were those of a man. Yet she spoke like an angel, eyes on the stars, of our kinship with the earth. Her low soothing voice made me feel that all was well.

Adept at getting others to do her bidding, Edith now had a devoted slave, dumpy and bristled, as housekeeper and dog's body. This was Miss Tucker who made date and walnut scones and cottage loaves, round and pale as herself. My aunt, 'Mistress of the Hives', provided the honey to be scooped from waxen combs on to our plates. Unquestioning we obeyed her rules of health, saving every scrap and peeling for the compost heap which steamed gently as a pudding alongside the garden fence. Subsequent summer visits found us picking fruit – first the hard, green, hairy gooseberries soon to be followed by jewelled clusters of red and black currants, more tedious to clean than to gather. Relief grew with the soft strawberries, raspberries and logans. My aunt had earned herself quite a name for her luscious strawberries, winning prizes whenever she exhibited them. Only later did I discover her secret. It happened that one day, after visiting the privy at the bottom of the garden I asked why in the absence of a chain, there was not even disinfectant. "Disinfectant!" she exclaimed, "And destroy all that rich living matter? Everything given is given back to the earth in *this* garden." Then seeing my puzzled look she went on. "Did you never guess why my strawberries are so big?" From then on I blessed the honey for tea which allowed me to refuse her home-made strawberry jam!

After these visits, return to Ribblesdale Place seemed an anticlimax. In rebellious mood I was taken for walks in the park by a governess who insisted that I wear gloves. My reaction was to throw them in the river. I felt like a plant

25

uprooted from a field, refusing to grow in a formal (and sooty) flower-bed. It was then that my mother made what was to be for us a momentous decision: she took a country cottage for the spring and summer – the indelible summer of our lives beginning with blossom and birdsong; ending with fallen apples in the orchard grass.

Chapter 2

Brock Cottage

A dusty white country lane, now the A6, winding between
hawthorn hedges, ran northwards between Preston and
Lancaster. Somewhere along this lane we turned on to the
Badger Bridge which led to a cluster of cottages and a farm
proudly known as Claughton-on-Brock. And here, under the
lee of the western Pennines, stood Brock Cottage which I still
return to in memories and dreams. Surrounded by meadows
and woodlands, its tall chimneys seemed to be growing out of
the ivy which wrapped it close as a tea-cosy. My mother led us
through a narrow white gate into another world. We found
ourselves walking beside a thick privet hedge shaped into
turrets to the front-door whose trellised porch was hung with
swathes of clematis and honeysuckle. Beyond the hedge was a
formal garden of square, crescent, and diamond-shaped beds
bordered with neatly trimmed box. There were vegetables,
flowers, and herbs including wallflowers, rosemary and
lavender, and much also to be discovered later. The lawn
beyond was springing with daffodils which straggled away
into an orchard. Here were damsons, plums and pears already
losing their blossoms, while gnarled apple trees, medallioned
with sage-grey lichen, were about to open pink-fisted buds.

27

On the north side of the orchard stood a well with a wooden roof from which hung a bucket and pulley. We leaned over the edge to gaze down into the black water shining up at us, black and sinister as a witch's eye. All the same, we were disappointed to hear that our drinking water would not be wound up from the well but drawn from a pump in the yard. Even this was more exciting than taps. And we were enchanted to find a privy with no chain – very private indeed, and well hidden from the house under a coat of ivy.

My mother had transformed the interior of a cold, dark and damp cottage with Persian rugs and flowered chintzes. There was an oak corner cupboard, and wheel-back chairs which she'd bought at the nearby Chipping chair factory for about one shilling each. The freshly white-washed walls were adorned with her mother's Worcester and Rockingham plates which I preferred to the Victorian water-colours of sheep and cows. Her treasured Dresden figures stood on shelves out of reach. That day a log fire flickered in the face of a warming-pan and enlivening brass candlesticks stood on either side the fireplace where trivet and fire-irons shone alive in the light.

The smell of burning wood mingled with the scent of polyanthus flowers crowding into a bowl on a gate-legged table. And over all there was a patient grandfather clock that ticked away the thrilling seconds. I flung my arms round my clever, pretty mother who had created something beyond the range of Aunt Edith. In my bedroom was white wallpaper with black polka dots; that night they were printed on my mind as I fell asleep, a late blackbird singing in my head.

Before the week was out we owned four hens, not in their first youth, each one known by name, who ate out of our hands, and produced three or four eggs each day all through the summer – thus showing appreciation of our loving care and nourishing scraps. My mother pumped our daily water-supply and ran the whole place till she engaged a gardener, Sam

Barnes, a kind man with big, capable hands and in his arms a rare thrust for digging. At first we shied away from him because of the strawberry mark on his face. Looked at from the reverse side he was handsome with the sun in his skin and eyes dark blue as cornflowers. Not only handsome, we were soon to find, but an ever-ready help in trouble.

April was already melting into May with a full burst of leaf and birdsong. Cuckoos, those bodiless voices, woke us at dawn to be followed by thrushes, blackbirds, dunnocks and robins which made every bush and tree a singing platform. Purple pyramids of lilac swayed by the front-door blowing away their heady scent. Beyond the garden, meadows rioted with wild flowers and every wood and hedgerow was misted in bluebells. Greedily we gathered fistfuls of violets, campion, stitchwort, filling our aprons with spring offerings to bring home and stuff into jugs and jam jars. There weren't enough vessels for the flowers which so soon wilted indoors. Nor were we short of a playmate. Fred Byers came every day from a nearby farm to the back-door. Sandy-haired, pale and freckled, he taught us to catch roach with a maggot speared on a bent pin. In the field surrounding the cottage were three ponds fringed with reed and wild-flags. Under a scum of green weed the stagnant water seethed with life. First we caught tadpoles to be brought home throbbing in jam-jars. There were minnows, eels and frogs, ready prey for Fred's nimble fingers which coaxed the slimiest creatures into his hold. We lined boxes with lily-pads – beds for the frogs which usually expired for lack of water. Fred scoffed at my squeamishness in handling a toad, the colour of rotted leaves, which squatted on my palm, eyes glistening black beads, throat pulsing like a swamp-bubble.

Fishing brought new delight into our days. It was Sam who equipped us with bamboo canes, a ball of string, a scarlet float and pin a-wriggle with its maggot. "Now you'll catch a salmon," he teased, "or maybe a shark." Thus encouraged, we sat for hours at the water's scummy edge watching the bubbles explode as from fermenting wine. Bloated flies glutted themselves on rotting vegetation; iridescent dragonflies rustled airily among dry reeds. One day we caught five roach and brought them home, shining silver on a cracked plate, for tea. Roach, fresh from the pond, gave us a fine scorn of white flabby cod and hake on the fishmonger's slab. Blissfully we sat and fished many a long day into twilight. Then came the day when Fred discovered a nest of five young blackbirds in a hawthorn bush beside the pond. Their wings already feathered, they were on the point of being fledged, and as we parted the thorny twigs, five yellow beaks opened wide in supplication. Suddenly Fred put his hand into the nest and threw the young birds, one by one, into the pond. I yelled, screamed, and clutched his arm to no avail. "You hateful beast!" I sobbed, watching the birds vainly beating their wings in the dark water. Never again would I fish with Fred, and weeks went by before I spoke to him. When he next came to the cottage I slammed the door in his face. This painful episode awoke many latent stirrings: hatred, compassion and regret.

Three weeks after our arrival my mother sat at breakfast reading a letter. With a sigh she put it down, and the first cloud arose. "Well my treasures," she began, "there's a surprise for you – a nice young French governess is coming here tomorrow." "Governess!" we echoed in dismay. And "Tomorrow!" "Yes," she smiled. "We can't let the whole summer slip by without lessons." And, yes, answering our clamour, Cécile, for that was her name, spoke perfect English. We were to have lessons in the annexe alongside the orchard. Elaine was nearly four, and didn't even know her letters. The year was at May, the sun shone, and our mother took us to Mrs Cookson's shop, the white cottage down the lane, to buy sweets, home-made, luxuries in war-time.

At four o'clock the following afternoon Mercer's black pony in the yellow-wheeled trap from Brock station two miles away, drew up at the gate. My mother, putting on her welcoming smile, hurried down the path to greet it. We fled to the orchard and crouched in the long grass. Before long, hearing her call, Elaine stood up in her blue cotton frock and gave the show away. My mother advanced towards us with a tall, slim, auburn-haired young woman. Cécile couldn't have been more than twenty, though to us she seemed quite old. But she was nice to look at in a dandelion-coloured dress. I most remember her small, even teeth and hazel-green eyes with brown flecks. And I remember a dimple on one side of her mouth when she smiled. We glared defiantly in answer to her friendly greeting. But she spoke in a low voice liltingly unlike the voices of other governesses: "Aren't you going to say 'ello?" No reply. My mother, telling her to take no notice, marched her back to the house.

Eventually, overcome by hunger, we slunk indoors. I sulked over the scones – my mother's were lighter and whiter than Miss Tucker's – feeling small and foolish with the ebbing of resentment. Already Cécile was melting us down, making me feel almost jealous that she was to sleep in Elaine's room. Next morning the sun, stronger each day now, beat through the annexe windows, playing upon faded spelling, geography, and history books. Apart from teaching us some basic phrases in French, Cécile devoted most of her time to helping Elaine, all golden hair and innocence, form laborious pothooks while I watched the big hand of the clock.

Twelve o'clock spelled freedom. While Elaine lagged behind with Cécile, I was off down the lane to Byers' farm – Fred was at school – to their dogs, cats, pigs and, best of all, their four horses. By now the milking cows were knee-deep in grass laced with sorrel and clover, foaming with a head of fool's parsley; only at milking time could I get near them to stroke flanks made silky with sun, calling each one by name: Silko, Cherry, Woodbine and Domino. There were stout plum-and-white Shorthorns, tan-and-white Ayrshires of the graceful curving horns, two deer-coloured Jerseys, and a couple of Friesians to make up the milk yield. At the dusty end of hot, sleepy afternoons Nap, the cow-dog, brindle-grey, wall-eyed, and supple as a lasso, would circle the twenty-acre field roping in the cattle, bunching them skilfully through the white six-barred gate. Then, master of the occasion, pink tongue lolling, he manoeuvred them with an odd nip and growl into the shippon yard. Each cow knowing her own stall hardly needed tying up for feeding and milking. Jim Byers, Fred's elder brother, and Tom, the farm-hand, brought three-legged stools on which they sat with heads pressed against the cow's side while they stroked and kneaded heavy udders, coaxing the milk to flow easily as for a calf.

Many an hour we watched this process, hypnotised by the strong spurts of milk against the pail's metal until the milk, creeping up the sides, began to purr gently, and bubble with froth. Half the milk, warm and creamy, was poured into tall cans in the cooling room where it awaited the next morning's supply for the milk-round. Meanwhile, half the remainder was set in wide wooden buckets for skimming off the cream, later to be hand-churned till it thickened into pale, cheesy farm butter. A great barrel-shaped container held the left-over milk to be broken into curds and whey for the calves. The chalk-white curds were tumbled in a metal vat, not unlike a washing-machine, and whirled round and round before being further broken up and squeezed free of liquid in powerful presses. The firm substance was then wrapped in cheese-cloths, tight as corsets, and set in large, fat wheels upon stone slabs to mature. Such Lancashire cheese, mild, creamy, and flavoured from clover and rye-grass, is not to be had today. Often after bedtime I would creep into the larder and cut a wedge to take upstairs.

Compared with the freedom enjoyed by the cows, Ramrod, the bull, endured a miserable existence in the dark fetid shed, fetlock-deep in straw manured by months of his captivity. He would thrust his powerful, triangular-shaped head over the open half-door and bellow the morning away, occasionally licking the brass ring in his nose with a pale pink India rubber tongue. What could be seen of his bulk was dark red, the colour of the curls tightly clustered around his short thick horns. Uneasy thoughts troubled me – for what reason did they keep him if he was a public danger, gave no milk, and wasn't sent to the slaughter-house? Then one day Jim led him forth with stick and chain attached to his nose-ring. "Where's he going?" I asked. " 'e's going a-visiting," Jim replied briefly walking him round the yard. "An' e's going to see 'is lady-love."

Huge and square, flesh and muscle rippling as he moved, he was a daunting sight. And those fearsome appendages suggested far fiercer goings-on than I had dreamed of in the summer-house. Suddenly I felt enormous concern for those gentle cows – no wonder they were sorrowful and meek.

Indeed, the mechanics of reproduction as learned on a farm fostered in me a fear of, even a distaste for all things male; compassion for the female. No wonder God was a man. And was that why, I asked myself, he had created Adam first. This attitude was reinforced by the antics of Shep, the sheep-dog, normally a lovable creature. There was nothing lovable in his mating with Sally, the springer-spaniel bitch. While he, forelegs clasped around her haunches, panted in full swing, all stops out, she gazed at me, her soft brown eyes mute and pleading. I ran for a bucket of water and flung it at him. "You hateful beast!" I sobbed, unable to pull him clear. "You get all the fun!"

That day at lunch I couldn't finish my pudding, and Cécile questioned me – " 'ave you been to Madame Cookson's?" she teased, and promised to take us for a picnic by the river that afternoon. The Brock, a rocky brown trout stream, ran past a water-driven flour mill about a mile away. We never tired of watching the water treadling the creaking wooden wheel used for grinding the corn, and so, on this hot day, we shouted for joy. My mother had gone to Garstang shopping, hiring Byers' trap for the purpose, and wouldn't be back till after tea. While Cécile was filling the picnic basket, Sam appeared at the back-door offering help. Standing there, tall and tanned, the 'strawberry' side of his face turned away, he looked strong and good. "Please, Cécile, let Sam come with us," we pleaded, but she gave him a smile and a firm "No." "Then I'll come an' 'elp carry t'tackle 'ome when I'm done 'ere," he nodded happily and turned back to the garden. I wondered why Cécile and Sam both dropped their h's.

Shoes and socks flung on the bank, we dug our toes in the river sand before daring the cold brown water. We ran our fingers through long tails of dark green weed, and peeled thick pads of moss from rocky slabs. Paddling among white-cupped water-crowfoot, we slipped shrieking from slippery stones, and in no time dresses, petticoats off, waded into deeper water. Cécile, skirt lifted, paddled alongside; all three intoxicated by the river smell and the warm scent of sun-soaked water-plants. We abandoned ourselves in elemental joys: water, air, earth and sun. Sun streaming through branches of alder, hazel and willow; shafting on leaf-dappled ledges of rock. Nearby the water-wheel creaked away, its sparkling crystal drips dripping into the river below.

There was no wind, and the wheel turned lazily while the engine in the mill throbbed in tune with the river. Greatly daring, we climbed the low wall enclosing the wheel, and gazed down and up as it revolved, mesmerised by its rhythm. All the world was in slow motion: river, wheel, and languid willows trailing pointed fingers in the water. Suddenly a kingfisher flashed upstream – sapphire torpedo, visitor from another planet. And now I spied a dipper, white shirt-front, fat and round as a golf-ball. Bobbing there on a flat stone, he might have been conducting an orchestra.

From the bank Cécile shouted that it was tea time. Eagerly we splashed to where she was laying out sandwiches, thermos, and a bottle of lemonade in a gap between trees. There, feet in the sand, backs to the sun we sat munching happily lulled by the peace of that untroubled world. Suddenly a dull thudding of hooves broke the spell. Alarmed, we turned round to see two vast hairy cart-horses, nostrils dilated, tails twitching, lumbering towards us. They jolted up to the bank and stamped to a halt. Then, thick necks outstretched, they snuffed at our picnic. Elaine's screaming made them even more inquisitive. Cécile waved her arms and yelled at them in French. As for me, the biggest coward, I backed into the river and collapsed on a stone. The biggest horse, a ragged rusty brown with a clown-white face gave a ludicrous buck, knocked over the mugs, and lipping among the food, selected a lump of cake. His companion, a grey, had fastened his teeth round the cork of a lemonade bottle, advanced ponderously down the bank towards Cécile, nipping playfully at her yellow dress, snatching a ribbon as a wisp of hay. We were spared the next act by Sam's tall figure emerging from the trees. Cécile wept with relief at the sight of him. Putting strong arms round the grey's neck, he coaxed him back up the bank and into the field. Then, slapping the haunches of the other, disposed of him too. Methodically he removed his boots and waded out to rescue me. Fortunately Cécile had brought a towel so that I was soon dry and wrapped in a cardigan. "Now then," soothed Sam after consoling Elaine, still red-faced and shaking, " 'ow about a nice cup o' tea?" He uncorked the thermos and poured the tea carefully into the three mugs, plopping two lumps of sugar in each. "Nothing like sugared tea for shock," he observed as we drank gratefully. Cécile gave him a rewarding smile and offered half her mug of tea, which he refused. Feet dried, shoes and socks on, we started for home like any family party with Sam carrying Elaine shoulder-high. He made jokes like a kind uncle till we reached the garden gate. Putting Elaine down gently, he nodded goodbye and strode away leaving Cecile gazing in wonder at his retreating figure.

After this she always gave Sam a friendly smile, and even offered to help him to weed the garden till my mother remarked at her sudden interest in the herbaceous border. One afternoon I surprised the two of them in the tool-shed; Sam's arm was around her waist as she selected a hoe. And I began to wonder at the frequent cups of tea she took out to him. My mother wondered even more when she found out that they had spent one whole evening together till long after dark, and from then on made sure that our three morning hours of lessons were uninterrupted. However, this relationship was of little interest to us whose lives were directed towards the fields and ponds and Byers' farm.

Mid-May saw the advent of shire stallions paraded along the lanes to serve various mares on their journeys. For this purpose these magnificent animals were decked out in festive style. Skins polished to satin; manes and tails braided with straw and ribbons; flower-studded, they strode out, necks arched, a brass bell jingling atop each forelock. Hugest of all was Blackthorn Blueblood, true to his name, a giant black, gleaming as fresh-cut coal, with white blaze and shining white fetlock feathers curling over polished ivory hooves. His mane and tail were plaited with royal blue ribbons, prided with cornflowers, while on his forelock tinkled a silver bell. King among horses, he was the pride and joy of the countryside, winner at shows, the goal of perfection for farmers seeking his service for their mares.

Such were the demands on him that only the best were

obliged. Old Frank Byers, father of the family, was downcast because Bess, his liver chestnut, failed to make the grade. Anyway, he was glad enough to accept the attention of Goldstone Forrester, a bright bronze-penny chestnut.

The day Goldstone visited the farm is engraved on my memory. His colours, emerald-green and primrose were flaunted gay as spring flowers. And as he advanced, pink nostrils flaring, head plunging from side to side, he skittered away from the leading-rein. Young and fresh, he was bubbling over with heady spring sap, ramping to prove his prowess. As he went by Elaine and I pressed ourselves into the bank, well clear of the hooves which struck sparks from the flinty road. Suddenly a Ford car – in those days a square tin rattle-box with a square brass front – clattered towards us. As it drew near, Goldstone, unused to traffic, snorted and backed into the middle of the road. Eyes rolling in terror, he reared up, lifting his leader from the ground. The Ford exploded to a halt, and the man tried to coax Goldstone past it. But as he came alongside he flattened his ears, and backed into a razor-sharp mudguard which slit open the fine skin of his haunch. A wound, eight inches long, gaped open like a pouch purse and slowly filled with blood which trickled darkly down his near hind leg. The stallion neighed in terror. After much soothing and stroking, he was eventually coaxed into one of the loose-boxes, and fresh straw was laid for him. There he stood, injured side sagging, slowly sweating away the afternoon in silent pain. There was nothing by which to gauge it but glazed eyes and sweat gradually darkening his entire body. Hours seemed to pass before the arrival of the vet when Jim hustled us from the stable and up to the barn where we waited, shivering in apprehension. Then came a muffled shot, and silence. I dared not imagine the scene in the stable and pushed it all from my mind till a van drew up and a man with ropes jumped down. There was talking next door and the thud of boots. Once again Jim appeared and set us on the road home. "Be away now," he ordered, "and stay at home till morning." I couldn't face tea, but Elaine, carrying a lighter weight of years, was soon putting her dolls to bed.

Another horror lay ahead at the farm. Since the drowning of the blackbirds we had kept clear of Fred, but the following Saturday he greeted us in the lane. "Come on sissies, an' see t'fun." Annoyance was overcome by curiosity. We followed him through the farm gate and alongside the sunken duck-pond whose dark, muddied sides were riddled with rat-holes. Squatting beside a hen-cabin, old Frank Byers, Jim and Tom, the farm-hand, were inspecting three cages. Tom opened one and drew out a fluffy chicken-yellow ferret. Eyes like pink glass beads, it squirmed around his hairy brown arms. "It's a beauty," he said lovingly, and introduced it to a rat-hole tunnelled under the nearest cabin. Meanwhile, Frank and Jim, each carrying a gun, accompanied by two fox-terriers, moved away to the far end of the rat run.

Apprehensively we waited, watching the men with guns lowered at the ready. In that heavy silence we hardly dared to breathe when suddenly a mud-coloured rat streaked out. Instantly it was savaged by one of the terriers. Then another, and another – each giving a shrill scream before we heard the soft crunch of bones in the terrier's mouth. A fourth was blown to rags by Jim's gun. Finally the ferret, Freddy, twitching his nose appeared at the entrance of the hole to be gathered up by Tom who replaced him in the cage. His paler, wirier young brother was popped down an adjacent hole with much the same result. But the next entrance led into the main rat run under the bank; this was explored by Rufus, the eldest and wiliest ferret of the three. He squirmed and sniffed before venturing inside, sliding on his stomach like a huge, sandy caterpillar. There was a long wait. And then – no fewer than six rats, two huge and fat, hurtled out to be torn up by the terriers or annihilated by the guns till the air smelt of fouled mud and gunpowder. But the heaviest rat had sunk its teeth into the smaller terrier's lip. In the ensuing struggle the dog flung the rat from side to side while blood streamed down his face. In the end Jim came to the rescue, knocking out the rat with the butt of his gun.

At the day's end, sixty-three rats hung by their tails from the clothes-line, later to be picked clean by magpies and crows. Orderly, indifferent nature is yet practical and law-abiding with no left-overs. Bluebottles would finish the job. Nor did Frank Byers hold with nursing weaklings to be a burden on the farm and a misery to themselves. "Let Nature sort 'em out," he would say, even at the loss of a pedigree calf. Just then, I interrupted him to ask how a rat could steal a hen's egg. He explained how the canny rat jumped into a nest-box, clasped the egg in its forepaws while a waiting partner seized its overhanging tail and gently pulled down the egg-bearing rat on to its back. "Why, rats is as crafty as 'uman beings," he said, "an' a deal better organised."

Thankfully we left this battlefield of mud and blood for the comfort of home. My mother, guessing us to be at the farm, had ceased worrying and cleared away the lunch which we couldn't, anyway, have eaten. Cécile was out, so she interrupted her brewing of nettle-beer to make our tea. Soon it was bedtime for Elaine's dolls, and I wandered out through the fields. It was evening in mid-June with thrushes and blackbirds nestling in the bushes, pausing every now and then for a last snatch of song. Ring-doves crooned among the tree-tops, and as I approached the roach's pond, the butterfly-yellow of flag flowers shone out. A mist of midges zoomed over the pond, driving me to the top of the field. Here a last year's haystack, sliced like ginger cake, stood invitingly warm in the evening sun. Burying my nose in the sweet scratchy hay, I crept round to the back. And there they were, lying on a loose bundle –

Cécile and Sam. She on her back, he turned towards her, one arm under her shoulders. He was looking at her as he looked at his prize roses, tracing the outline of her wide mouth with a forefinger – the same strong, gentle forefinger that pricked out his seedlings. Wholly absorbed, he didn't see me, but the look on his face made me feel like a trespasser. Here was something beyond my small experience, something that couldn't be told.

Softly I crept away over the fields where jagged shadows were lengthening under the trees. I climbed into the orchard breathing in the smell of damp earth and leaves, hugging a secret to myself. Too young to ask what life was about, I knew it was something good.

Chapter 3

Summer Idyll and Return

Midsummer 1916 came in hot and dry with the meadow grass too tall to wade through. Lessons, in Alice-in-Wonderland fashion, were apt to lessen from day to day. Governess instruction was a poor substitute for the high school, and Cécile's attention was divided between Elaine's pot-hooks and Sam's pauses in gardening which, unlike lessons, lengthened daily. Midday – signal for release and his dinner hour – found us running over the fields. While Cécile lingered over our books, Sam hovered by the annexe door.

We spent long evenings at the pond with midges biting us energetically. My mother used to worry when we came home late and I noticed a certain restraint in her manner towards Cécile whose evenings out were becoming longer and more frequent. One hot night I couldn't sleep and crept into Elaine's room to find Cécile's bed empty. The clock chimed, and feeling uneasy I tip-toed barefoot downstairs, walking as on moss so as not to disturb my mother whom I spied in the sitting-room reading under a lamp. In the kitchen cupboard I found my slippers, put them on and, wearing a dressing gown, made my way past the roach pond to the cut-into haystack to which instinct had led me. There behind the haystack they lay entwined, Sam and Cécile, heedless of the world around them. The earth seemed to draw a long breath; nearby a disturbed blackbird whistled fresh and clear as a new-peeled stick of willow. I returned to the cottage, my nightie trailing in the long dew-heavy grass. The young moon, fine as an illuminated finger-nail, lay on her back.

Next morning, Cécile had a dewy look, moonlight in her eyes. She seemed unaware of my mother's reproachful silence over lunch, but volunteered to take us out of her way – for another picnic. "I know what that means," she shook her head. There was a sense of strain about my mother these days with my father away for such long periods. He came home only three times in four years; moreover only part of his Army pay came home so that money worries were added to responsibility for our family home and my father's medical practice. Yet, though physically delicate, she was infinitely resourceful and managed to transform a frugal way of life into a summer idyll. Every left-over scrap went to the rewarding hens; we fetched milk in cans from the farm at a penny a pint, and strong, cheesy butter at eight-pence a pound. Sam brought us many a young rabbit which my mother would fry with herbs, onions and carrots – all home-grown – making a most delicious meal. With boiling-fowls to be had for a shilling or so, and our fresh-caught roach, food cost us next to nothing. I was bidden to gather young nettles and wore gloves for this hated task. My mother insisted they tasted better than spinach, and were useful, too, for her nettle-beer, brown and clear as a trout stream. Apart from this, she baked bread and cakes, made lemon-cheese, jam and all our clothes.

On this particular afternoon, having refused Cécile's offer of a picnic, she decided to take us to see her younger sister, Mab, married to Harry Astley-Bell, a successful cotton magnate. They lived at Sullom End, three miles north of Brock Cottage, in a big new house on the flank of Sullom Hill, so called because, centuries ago, its cairn was used by Druid sun-worshippers. Hopefully we set out, my gallant mother pushing Elaine in the go-cart. The way led through a dim green tunnel of beeches, branches interlacing overhead, whose pale grey trunks were massive as cathedral pillars and here it was silent and dark as in a cathedral. When we emerged into daylight, an unfriendly wind was tossing a ball of cloud, unrolling it like wool across the sun. Without warning a sudden cold rain lashed out at us, bending branches and thrashing the leaves as we went by. Elaine started to howl; I whined to go back but my mother, already flagging, plodded on. "We're more than half-way there," she said. But the last lap, a long steep hill, nearly finished her. White-faced exhausted and soaked, she rang the front door bell. It was answered by a neat parlour-maid in a black poplin dress, white-frilled muslin cap and apron. "Oh, Ma'am!" she cried in dismay when my mother explained who she was. "Do come in, now. The mistress won't half be upset."

We stood, the three of us, making rain puddles on the oak parquet flooring of the hall when Aunt Mab appeared, warm with welcome and reassurance. She was the sort of person who made you feel that all must be well. Tall, gracious, full-bosomed, she was a regal figure overflowing with confidence and charm. My mother was bustled away to the guest-room while we found ourselves in the nursery suite and its warm, tiled bathroom smelling of lavender powder and Pears' soap. This region was under the domination of the fearsome Nanny, dark, bespectacled and lame, armoured in the shiny starch of cuffs, cap and belt. In no time our wet clothes were whipped off and we wallowed in a slippery, steaming bath, so different from the dingy tin tub of the cottage.

Dressed in borrowed clothes we found ourselves on a rug beside the brass-railed guard of a lively fire. Never had I seen such glossy lumps of coal as in that gleaming brass scuttle. Nor such polished linoleum, so white and woolly a rug.

43

Everything, from nanny's cap and apron to the paintwork, nursery china and tea-cloth, sparkled like snow in the sun. Tiny flames gleamed in the pictures, on plates and mugs; quivered along the bars of a cage where a canary, heedless of the rain outside, was pulsing in song. It was like a page in a brand-new book of nursery tales. The book became alive with the children who, silent and watchful so far, suddenly pelted us with questions. Enid, with her long, shining red hair and bright blue eyes, had a quicksilver mind so that my hesitant answers fell away below her needling curiosity. "Slow! Slow!" sang six-year-old Meyrick, equally blue-eyed, laughing as he chased me round the table. Meanwhile, Elaine the youngest, sat blissfully combing the sheepskin rug with fat fingers. Nanny rescued me from the persecution of her beloved charges and soon we were devouring boiled eggs and thin white bread and butter.

After tea, hands and faces washed, hair brushed, we were sent down to the drawing-room where my mother and Aunt Mab sat talking. My aunt was larger than my mother in every way, more expansive, assured and talkative. I later learned that the generous bust was due to exercising a fine contralto voice, heard at concerts all over the county, which had earned her the title of 'Blackburn's Clara Butt'.[17] After half an hour's talk tuned-down to us children, she pressed a bell for the parlour-maid who was asked to ring for the chauffeur who, in turn, was bidden to drive us back home in the soigné black Daimler – certainly a more comfortable way of travelling than Aunt Edith's pony-cart.

Next day, the first of July 1916, sparkled bright as a blue diamond and after lessons we begged for a picnic beside the river. This time my mother came with us, and Cécile glancing back at Sam, carried the baskets. Our way led through an avenue of limes to Scrambler's farm, the richest in the district.

[17] Dame Clara Ellen Butt, British contralto and concert singer, 1872-1936.

As we turned into the yard we were assaulted by hideous screams and there in front of the farmhouse, a pig was being roped struggling onto a stout, low wooden table. We were in time to see the flash of steel as one of the two men in attendance plunged a knife into the pig's jugular vein. The screams, intensified with a jet of blood spurting upwards, were instantly muted to gurgles and blood-bubblings while the pig quivered and twitched upon the table. My own scream was drowned in the universal cry of fifty-nine other pigs mad with fear, waiting for slaughter, battering against the door that imprisoned them. Overcome by horror and the bright crimson of that life-blood spilled on the cobbles, I raced back down the avenue, fingers in my ears. The others followed and found me sitting under the weir which roared and foamed under the nearby bridge. White foam and roar to wash out the sight and sound of slaughter. Here the water drowned the death-cries of fifty-nine pigs. I refused to budge from the plunging river stinging us with clean, cold spray. So we sat in enforced silence on a bank harsh with nettles and thistles. Cécile and my mother struggled with the picnic, shouting at each other above the raging torrent, but while they poured out shaking cups of tea on the slope, I refused to eat.

I also refused to return through the farm, where my mother wanted to see Mrs Scrambler, until Cécile had been back to make sure that the killing was over. As we approached, an ominous hush fell. Men's voices and laughter faded as we paused outside an open door. Inside, lining a long, narrow building, hanging upside-down from steel hooks, were sixty pig corpses. Mouths and eyes open, scalded, scraped, stomachs slit down the middle, they hung stiff and white as wax. They looked like effigies from Madam Tussauds or prizes in butchers' shops. A smell of scrubbed wood, hair and lard pervaded the mortuary atmosphere of terrible marble stillness. Fixed in the doorway I out-stared my longing not to look, which might have resulted in even worse imagined horrors through the night.

Since that day, I have never liked pork or veal or any meat white from such hateful blood-letting. Ironically, while those pigs were being slaughtered, the entire British Army in France was advancing in the first of the bloody battles of the Somme. All our resources and what were available of the French were thrown into that summer-long struggle. Every day my mother bent anxiously over the *Lancashire Evening Post* and on the next day after this episode the banner headline was printed on my mind because it was July 2nd 1916 and Elaine's fourth birthday. The great black letters spelled out: *British Attack on the Somme*. While fixing four candles on Elaine's cake, my mother, answering my curiosity, told me of enemy losses, the capture of German prisoners and guns. Vaguely during that summer, so wonderful here, so terrible over there in Flanders mud, I registered other black newsprint; *British Advance*; *Bombardment of the British*, and the Army's appeal: *Send More Stuff*. It was all too remote and removed from our bright days which ran colourful as beads on a thread: a flower-filled garden, meals outdoors, hay time, harvest, and sun over all.

When August came in with a great gold harvest-moon, we could hardly believe that along the south-east coast nightmare zeppelins were dropping their poisoned eggs, venturing as near as the mouth of the Thames. Our ears were filled with the sound of the reaping-machine as Bess, Byers' chestnut mare, partnered by Brock, the bay, strode proudly alongside rustling acres of oats. Rhythmically the tall corn fell in swathes to be gathered, bound and corded by that magical machine. The men arranged them into stooks of three – like ballet dancers, heads and hands a-droop, after the movement of summer. "And to think of those stacks and stacks of dead soldiers," my mother sighed and shook her head. We read about people who were starving or living on musty bread unfit for cattle, but such misery was impossible to imagine among all this golden peace and plenty. Yet even that was to be invaded; Jim Byers and Tom had received their call-up papers and were off next morning leaving old Frank in charge with a lame hired man. Sam, for some reason, wasn't called up so he offered his services to the farm while still managing, most days, to slip back to our garden where Cécile had undertaken to work in his absence.

War or no war, the two of them grew brown and happy as the harvest. Then one morning, more radiant than ever, she announced that she and Sam were to be married. My mother, saying nothing, said all. That night she wrote a long letter to my father; she must have felt lonely and left-out with two lovers and two children for company, and such a weight on her shoulders. But at the time I was unable to share her sadness. However, there was one incident which did bring something of the war's grief home to me. Early in September I went as usual to Byers' farm for the milk and was surprised not to see the quart can standing ready filled on the shelf by the back door. Funny that Mrs Byers should have forgotten after so many months. I hesitated on the threshold and heard from the kitchen a sound of sobbing. A terrible, tearing, shaking sound which made me want to run away. But something compelled me to stay and to venture inside. Mrs Byers, hands to her face, was swaying back and forth in the rocking chair by the window while weeping with silent pauses between the gulping sobs that seemed to break her apart. She saw me standing there helpless, afraid to speak, but took no notice except to cry out, "Oh, Jim! Jim! Jim!" as she screwed up the orange envelope in her lap. When she began to moan like an animal, I turned and fled.

There is something indecent, shocking to a child in a grown-up's grief. Grown-ups should be brave and strong as they tell us to be. Such unmasking is against proper behaviour. In a

47

whirl of mixed up emotions, including anger, I raced back home as though I'd been assaulted. Indeed, my feelings had been assaulted and I poured out everything to my mother who completely understood, soothed my fears, and tried to explain. But for the first time I felt frightened of life.

That must have been a fearful summer for all those outside the safety of innocence and green fields. At the time of the many battles of the Somme, the war-machine sucked in every young, fit man available, sent them after a mere fortnight's drilling into the front line where the average life of an infantryman was twenty minutes. Jim, cutting the corn at the beginning of August, was himself cut down before the month was out. How fortunate were Elaine and I to find so much happiness, without guilt, in 1916 with the crops ripening and green apples plentiful on the orchard trees.

In September the chapter ended and we returned home to hear that three German airships were circling London while a zeppelin had fallen in flames. It seemed an unreal world until Middlehurst — my father's 'right hand man' — faced us with happenings 'over there'. Invalided home from the Gunners, he had been badly wounded; we were dismayed to see him in pale blue uniform, head bandaged and arm in splints. Yet his blue eyes laughed with us as before and he enlivened us with 'terrible tales from the trenches'. And, his marvellous optimism justified, he was twice more to go over the top, enduring the entire war till it crawled and exploded to its muddy, bloody end. My father's chauffeur, Bardell, even luckier, actually survived over four years of shells, bombs, guns and gas without a single scratch.

Our home, without my father, seemed strangely quiet — no sense of expectancy and crisis, very few patients. I was thankful to be returned to the High School where I enjoyed every moment of the day except for that noisy half-hour in the parrot-cage of an asphalt playground. Reading and writing came a close second to the joys of the countryside; and after a brain-fallow summer, getting into a book was like dipping into a well. Food had become ever scarcer, so tea-parties were cut out; Jim and Harry finally discouraged from calling. Throughout that winter and the following spring my mother was far from her usual self. Her three nights a week at the station buffet had to be abandoned because of bouts of sickness and indigestion. When during the following summer my father came back on his last leave, he was deeply concerned and suggested that she should take rooms in 'Blackpool-of-the-champagne-air'. A change of environment away from duty calls, he hoped, would do her good. Accordingly, in September 1917, to Blackpool we duly went, I regretfully saying farewell to the High School and taking an instant dislike to the concrete, treeless 'pleasure ground' whose strong cold winds seemed to bite into your very thoughts.

Worst of all, we were sent to a kind of dame's school whose headmistress, Miss Lofthouse, was like a character from Dickens. Tall and thin, wearing pince-nez, she covered her angles with flouncy dresses which trailed in a peacock's tail behind her. Her dark, smooth hair was scraped back and she wore a black velvet neckband to offset an 'Annie Laurie' neck, curving and long, if not white 'like the swan'. Miss Lofthouse governed by ruler and iron; the former in her ever-ready hand; the latter in her soul. We children had to wear silly, frilly dresses – pink for fair girls, yellow for dark, and heaven help the in-betweens – and long white socks and ankle-strap shoes. Rewards and punishments were meted out according to behaviour, never for academic achievement; if you were good you got a red bead; not so good a yellow one. Black was for misconduct, which included not bowing when Miss Lofthouse appeared in the morning. In three wretched months I received three yellow beads; the rest were black. Queen-like, Miss

49

Lofthouse stood on a platform offering a bead to each girl who filed past below. Name and colour were trumpeted by Miss Toogood, deputy head. This ceremony absorbed precious time, as did the early morning chorus of "Good-morning, Miss Lofthouse!" accompanied by low curtseys, and "Good-morning, girls!" from the platform, followed by ridiculous rituals with our 'queen' enthroned in a carved oak chair. After a questionnaire on yesterday's behaviour and a tirade on morals and resolutions came the school song adulating the headmistress and thumping to a close with: "I'm going to be a good girl today!" If we learned anything beyond bowing, curtseying and elocution, I have forgotten it. What a fertile 'anti-establishment' seed-bed!

We returned home for Christmas and, in the excitement of presents and stirring war-time puddings, forgot my father's absence. Kate, now our only maid, filled the kitchen with *It's a Long Way to Tipperary* and *Keep the Home Fires Burning* and, defying orders, she threw a shovelful of coal, collected from the station yard, on the fire. "The Germans won't be freezing us out at all, at all!" she laughed.

The war was dragging on with lengthening casualty lists and my mother looked pale and anxious but, eight days before Christmas, she waved the newspaper over the breakfast-table. The banner headline read: *Entry into Jerusalem*. Propping it against the milk-jug she read to us: " 'Allenby proceeds on foot through the city. Women strew the streets with flowers.' – It sounds like Palm Sunday," she added. While she was absorbed with war news we could think of nothing but Christmas and the snow.

Snow came thick and early that winter, muffling trees and houses; padding the roofs with silence. A spiked finger pierced the crusty white collar of the sundial. For days we were marooned, and Kate set to with makeshift baking, attempting bread and pies with grey flour. "And to think we're being told to eat less," she laughed, twirling the roiling-pin. Indeed, the papers were full of the food shortage with Lord Robert Cecil warning us that food waste would prolong the war. There was no waste in our household of thrift; margarine papers were scraped with a knife; acorns ground up for an unappetising drink sweetened with saccharin. We were thankful for the eggs pickled from Brock Cottage – these, with fried bacon-rinds, were a special Sunday treat.

In spite of the general food shortage that Christmas, Aunt Mab had somehow persuaded her cook to bake a cake for my father. This she posted in November 1917 and in return received a letter from him dated January 27th 1918, from the 44th Stationary Hospital, Vantara, describing shuttlecock travels between Alexandria, Vantara, Jaffa and Cairo to set up research laboratories on cholera.

Chapter 4

Boarding School

Unable to find anyone to maintain the practice, harassed by money troubles and two quarrelling daughters, my mother's health continued downhill with increasing bouts of sickness and pain. It happened at this time that her eldest sister, Edie, had come to live in Birkdale – about twenty miles away from us – where there were many girls' boarding schools. Anxious about my mother, Edie suggested that we should be sent to one of these schools, inexpensive for the convenience of clergymen and doctors, where she might keep an eye on us.

So it was arranged, and this thoughtful aunt provided my mother, too ill to travel by train, with a hired car for the journey. This enormous extravagance, to our way of thinking, was fully justified because on the way my mother was so ill that, instead of returning home, the car took her to hospital. There she had an emergency operation for appendicitis, the then 'fashionable' disease. We hoped this would end her health troubles which were too much to be borne alongside the bleak new life ahead of us.

Early memories of Pincroft School are blurred by the struggle for survival and abysmal homesickness. Here we endured a life at the opposite pole from Miss Lofthouse with her frills and curtseys.[18] The headmistress, Miss Sharp, true to her name, scorned everything soft, pretty and comfortable. Hers was a poker-down-the-back regime of cold bedrooms, scant food and long walks. Girls must stand upright, sit upright, and be upright. Our diet consisted mainly of bread-and-margarine, cold water, and the Scriptures, the main rule being: "Thou shalt not." Most things one wished to do were wrong; virtue lay in achieving what you most hated doing such as breaking the ice in tall bedroom ewers for the winter morning top-wash. Hard chairs, hard beds and scant rations were good for the soul; lumps in porridge and cold baths were considered suitable chastening for the offspring of doctors and clergy.

In September, 1918, Elaine, aged six, was the youngest in the school – the fair-haired baby to be taken under the wing of Miss Grayson, the pretty second head who lavished on her a store of unspent affection. I, three years older and the next youngest, moved unprotected in a hostile world, shut out by Miss Grayson lest I impinge on her new baby, disliked by Miss Sharp with her fine nose for rebellion, ignored by the other staff. Soon I learned to stand on my own feet, dispelling the myth that the boarding-school child is protected. Here one had to fight for the merest privilege of a margarined crust – the only part of the loaf worth eating – which was hotly competed for. Even to pull off this prize might earn the spite of the other girls so one learned to be canny. Like a babble of hungry rooks in our black lisle stockings, we set up a Council for the Crusts. There were eight of these to a loaf, the top and bottom slices being cut into four. Considering that tea and supper consisted solely of bread-and-marge, breakfast almost so – with the addition of one teaspoonful of marmalade, one ladle of porridge – the division of crusts was vital. Even for wartime and its aftermath of greater shortages with no fresh fruit or

[18] Miss Lofthouse, Headmistress, Dame's school in Blackpool.

53

vegetables, our diet fell way below prison fare. Protein appeared only at mid-day dinner when we had one tablespoonful of stew or mince, one slice of roast meat on Sunday, and on Friday the invariable cod hidden in a mainly potato fish-pie.

Small wonder we grew anaemic and spotty, suffered frequent colds and headaches, and the blight of Pincroft: Constipation. To combat this nuisance, Miss Sharp and Matron instituted the Liquorice Parade. Every Friday evening after our cementing supper we joined the liquorice-powder line-up. This foul, dingy, khaki-coloured liquid certainly set the lavatories flushing on Saturday mornings – our games and matches day – in the plot designed so that no girl would need to be excused the dreaded Sunday churchgoing.

The word 'Sunday' sounded a knell. At 9.45, wearing straw boaters (boards) we set forth in crocodile to walk the two miles to St. Andrews, Southport. Those matins with three psalms, four hymns, the litany and the lot, including a twenty-five minute sermon, gave us a distorted taste of eternity, which never afterwards seemed to be a desirable state. Added to the misery of the service, I nearly always fainted during the psalms when hot green waves of nausea washed over me till I passed out. I dreaded coming round in a dark, dusty pew and being pulled up to sit it out till the end. In vain I pleaded with Miss Sharp to be excused church. I was compelled to sit with her on the back row where the wide brim of my board prevented me from leaning against the wall. Wet or fine we plodded to church, umbrellas and wellingtons complete in bad weather. We concluded that Miss Sharp had a crush on the vicar, the only person with whom she became human.

Not all was grim. Ten to twelve-year-olds compelled to be in bed at six o'clock with lights out and no talking reap their own rewards. The moment the staff and seniors were in supper our day began; we listened to each others' life-stories, richly

54

embroidered, played games and in summer tiptoed barefoot down the forbidden front stairs – an ideal setting for the church services by which we parodied the Sunday ritual. Valerie, a vicar's daughter, played parson in white calico nightie and black stockings for stole. She conducted baptisms, weddings, funerals – for which the smallest girl was laid out in a drawer. Madge acted scout, and when supper was over she raced on stage hissing: "Chairs!" This was our signal for retreat. Back in bed we recalled our most horrifying experiences all of which were excelled by those of Mildred, a sprightly, dark-eyed girl with a huge appetite for drama. At eleven she was the only one to have a boyfriend. And she knew all the ropes. Fascinated and aghast, we listened to her description of how 'IT' happened. We squirmed and secretly disbelieved. "Only animals do that," objected someone. "Ah," replied the wise one, "but man is an animal. And he had the largest you-know-what in the whole animal kingdom." We sighed for the realms into which we could not follow her, and turned to more interesting topics such as ghosts and murders.

At thirteen Mildred was the sharpest, wittiest girl in Form III. It was she who sprinkled sawdust on the grey head of Miss Dickie, standing behind her as she sat taking the history class. And when Miss Dickie bent over her desk in a shower of dust, Mildred was ready with the duster, flicking joyously at her bun till every hair pin fell out. Mildred stooped to gather them up, handing them back in the light of praise and gratitude. After that she was always top in history. Far more, she was foremost in everything: limericks, dirty stories, nicknames for staff. Added to which she excelled in mimicry and parody. In Form III Mildred was also, and foreseeably, first with 'the curse'. Enviously we watched her flat chest – she was skinny as a monkey – rounding out nicely, filling her blouse. One Saturday evening she bounced nose-in-air into the bedroom, a packet of sanitary towels under one arm, a parcel in hand. "Guess what, chaps!" she announced stripping the paper off a cumbersome bust-bodice and fitting it like armour plate over her dress. Doubled up with giggles, we were at the same time filled with awe and admiration. "I can have a baby, now," she laughed, "but I'd rather have fun – up with Marie Stopes!"[19]

Mildred, the irrepressible, had no respect for anyone except a hefty girl whose surname was Gladstone, great-niece of the Great Man, with whom she conspired and consorted. It was these two who had locked Elaine and me in a wardrobe on our first night at school – a practice considered suitable as an initiation for new bugs. However, after this unpromising start I gradually pulled up, if not to Mildred's level at least to her toleration. Eventually we became friends, moving up the school together, disliked by most of the staff, detested by Miss Sharp. For instance, one Saturday, after an outing with my mother and during the polite goodbyes, Miss Sharp caught me stuffing a slab of chocolate up my knicker leg, yet laughed it off in my mother's face. "Oh well," she sympathised, "they will do these things." As soon as my mother was gone she rounded on me: "How dare you, you deceitful girl? Give me the chocolate at once. And you'll go without sweets for the rest of the term." Considering our allowance was two sweets on Saturdays, two on Sundays, exactly doled out, this may not seem a severe punishment. But it was the only gastronomic pleasure, in school, we had.

Pincroft punishments were more subtle than the ruler raps of Miss Lofthouse: you might be put in silence for a week; any girl caught even whispering to you was likewise penalised. No games, gym, or supper were common rewards of ill-doing. Reading forbidden books resulted in learning portions of Scripture by heart. Elaine, when only six years old, was given twenty lines for forgetting to wear a dressing-cape during the

[19.] Marie Stopes – British author, campaigner for women's rights, pioneer in family planning, 1880-1958.

ritual tooth-combing of hair against nits. Anyone over nine was liable for a hundred or more. An enterprising member of staff might order us to say the alphabet or the books of the Bible backward, to recite the thirteen times table or a Shakespeare sonnet. Such punishments were not sadistic – any more than pouring a jug of cold water over a girl having hysterics. We suffered more sorely at the hands of the girls themselves: there was Brenda, square, strong and very plain who threatened to smother any small girl who annoyed her, and Priscilla with her compass stabbing an enemy in the back. Precious hot-water bottles (our one winter comfort) were hidden or unstoppered in bed, pebbles substituted for sweets and, on one occasion, a fish-hook twisted into a woolly vest. None of these pranks could be reported to the staff, for fear of worse persecution. However, shared hardship breeds comradeship; a supperless girl invariably received a smuggled crust, to be savoured under the bedclothes.

As to clothing, we wore navy gym-slips but, apart from finer ones for Sunday, we wore nothing else – days, evenings and all seasons alike. We were driven to take dancing classes for the sheer pleasure of wearing another kind of dress. Green blouses, flannel or poplin according to season, were also unvaried, as were the navy blue overcoats and boys' caps to match. Underneath, unlovely liberty bodices, knicker-linings and bloomers completed the outfit. To add to this seductive get-up were squares of unhemmed calico – nose-rags – in lieu of handkerchiefs. No doubt, being burnable, they coped with our perpetual colds, albeit scratchy for raw noses. Every three weeks Miss Prime came to wash our hair, dried upside down in front of an open, often smoky, coal fire. Under such conditions it was amazing that any girl managed to look attractive. But we had our beauties – lovely Lorna of the long gold hair, worshipped by us juniors as she performed her end-of-term Spring Dance with the grace of Persephone. Then there was Norma, the red-head, fleet as Atalanta,[20] winning the hundred yards with yards to spare in our summer sports – an occasion of joy, synonymous with long hot days on the tennis-courts. This was the Big Day of the year with the steep, warm-scented grass banks, white with daises. From here proud parents viewed our prowess while Miss Sharp, diminished for once, smiled and nodded approval in the midst. For today she was powerless to forbid our rare, therefore heightened ecstasies. Oh, the winning of the three-legged, the flower-pot and sack races! Only one degree less in glory than the winning of the high jump the day Peggy Irwin, at thirteen, topped five feet. All this to be rewarded by a super tea of powdered lemonade and cream buns.

But such events, during that painful first term, were undreamed of. The second, miscalled spring, term was far worse. I was even more homesick after the first terrible novelty had worn off. January brought chills, chilblains and cold classrooms. Between classes we fought for places on lukewarm radiators – a practice not only severely punished but threatened, by Matron, with lifelong piles. At night we hurried to bed, unwashed, wearing vests and bed socks after a supper of bread-and-marge. When the 'rising' bell sounded at 7.10, our hearts sank amid thoughts of icy water and cold linoleum. I was often ill with a return of earache and abscesses but Miss Sharp said that I was lucky not to be a donkey with such long ears. As Mildred remarked, her sense of humour was feeble.

Perhaps it was deficiency in humour, rather than severity, which made her classes so unrewarding. We had to pay attention because we were scared of her. Only the day-girls, safely home at four o'clock, were relaxed in her presence. But learning without humour is dead, and Miss Sharp's teaching was uninspired. She took us for French and Scripture – in which she excelled, appearing to have the Bible by heart. But

[20] Atalanta. Described as a goddess per Greek legend.

58

our spirits sank at her appearance. Sometimes the strain was intolerable. Poor Valerie shrank like a rabbit in her glare: "You, a vicar's daughter, cannot recall the Transfiguration!" Her cold blue eyes alighted on me, and I started with Christ going up into a high mountain. Then some demon of perversity got into me – dare I say it – and I continued in a small, flat voice: "And his garments were made exceeding white, whiter than any Pullar from Perth could white them!" There was a fearful hush, a strangled giggle, and Miss Sharp stiffened in disbelief before the lava of her wrath descended upon me. I was in total disgrace. Outlawed, on the brink of expulsion, I became her No.1 unfavoured pupil.

In spite of all I enjoyed learning – even lessons, especially English, and after a drilling in the Border Ballads, I discovered a knack for writing verse. Words became a fascination, leaping into scansion and rhyme, making patterns and colours. I won all the competitions and, to Miss Sharp's chagrin, one of my efforts was read out by the vicar at the end-of-term prize-giving. It seemed so easy, and I soon learned that this faculty had nothing to do with being clever, but was merely something that happened – not because of, but in spite of one-self. But in the third form I earned a false reputation for braininess based largely on a photographic memory. To be in the top three in English, History, Scripture and such subjects was simply a matter of opening the text book and printing it in your mind. The difficulty lay in transposing the material into my own words. When I was fourteen I had the entire Greek History set by heart, thus gaining 98% in the final exam. I used to infuriate the others, in an attempt to enliven our dreary crocodile walks, by reciting Macaulay's *Lays of Ancient Rome*. We began this exercise taking turns but after about the twentieth stanza even Mildred packed up, and I, hateful show-off, insisted on carrying on.

During this period was the added incentive of my 'pash' for

Miss Marks, English and History mistress, who illuminated for us the Romantic Poets, especially Tennyson.[21] She charged Greek History with such life and meaning that I believed myself to be the reincarnation of a Greek nymph – an idea since modified to that of slave. There seemed something strange in the way I could answer questions about uncovered ground. None of us learned a word of Greek, but one day Miss Marks asked for a two-word title, supposing we had written a book about the Greek army's final descent upon Marathon after weeks of wandering in the mountains. Without thinking I put up my arm and said: "Thalassa! Thalassa!"[22]

Quick-wit Mildred was sharper and cleverer than I, excelling at Algebra and English Grammar. Then there was Sybil – later to become a barrister – enigmatic as her name implied, sitting silent, absorbing everything. With her wise-comic face she had it over all fifteen of us in those hotly competitive classes. Another love was for the piano. My over-zealous teacher imagined I had the makings of a concert pianist – this after I played in a Carnegie Hall concert. But my lop-sided brain too often let us down. Stabbing my knuckles with a sharp pencil, she once exclaimed in despair: "I can't understand you – one day you are my most intelligent pupil; the next you are the most stupid!" Part of the trouble was poor sight-reading. I played everything from memory. However, an open competition provided an opportunity for combining the two. All entrants were given a two-page piece of music which was to be learned, honour-bound, away from the piano. The great day came with about forty nervous competitors sitting in front of a large audience. I listened amazed as girl after girl failed to produce more than a bar or two. Since my name began with 'R', I was late to be called, and became increasingly

[21] Alfred Lord Tennyson – British Poet Laureate, 1809-1892.
[22] Thalassa per Greek mythology, a primordial sea goddess, daughter of Aether and Hemera.

apprehensive with every failure. Shaking when my turn came, I sat on the stool, recalled the music on the page, and played it through without a fault. It felt strange applying this stored impression to the keyboard. But it was so easy. My pleasure in winning the competition was dimmed by the belief – among girls and staff alike – that I had cheated and secretly played the piece beforehand on the piano. I couldn't make them understand that for me such a competition was a piece of cake.

At Pincroft, as must now be plain, the spirit of competition was encouraged in order to get the best and the most out of us. A method which works wonders for the top half of the class, but may not work at all for the rest, though I remember a fighting spirit not to be bottom. Indeed, to be 'next to bottom' was a triumph in reverse. As to the more academic girls despising the others, there was none of this at Pincroft. On the contrary, the most popular girls were almost always those who did not excel in class, they were admired for not being 'swots', for their independence, excellence at games, good humour, good looks, cunning in avoiding forfeits, or for other and more interesting qualities. In short, academic competition existed, but only among the academic; there was never any suggestion, as is so feared today, of one type of girl feeling inferior to another. Children feel a deeper sense of inferiority for some physical defect such as a limp, a squint, fat legs or a spotty face which cause far more agony than being bottom in arithmetic. The Creator has much to answer for.

Pincroft's excellent results in the School Certificate examinations (then Oxford and Cambridge Senior and Junior Locals) were achieved by competition, a well-qualified staff and small classes – never more than fifteen – in a school of 120 girls. And probably Miss Sharp's exhortations (greeted with derision) did some good: "If a thing's to be done, it must be well done." And her methods speak not unfavourably for a certain degree of fear – awe, even. We learned that it paid to do as we were told with certain exceptions. It was helpful to have a framework of rules against which, occasionally, to rebel. Spartan in all ways, Miss Sharp expected us to follow her example: cold baths, scant food and clothing, long walks and exercises were applauded. Never ill herself, she lacked all sympathy for our frailties. For instance, a delicate ten-year-old, after a midsummer school outing – without a hat – among the burning Birkdale sand hills, got sunstroke and was dead before midnight. And after a virulent bout of chicken-pox I was ordered to scratch off the scabs that stuck like limpets to my face. I obeyed, and for five years was pock-marked in true Elizabethan fashion. Another time, feeling very ill, I knocked timidly on her door. "And what's the matter with you?" she asked, fingers locked, thumbs butting together in characteristic fashion. "Please, Miss Sharp, I feel sick," and "Be sick, then!" was her tart reply. Disciple of Émile Coué,[23] one might say that she forbade us to be ill. Rarely indeed was a doctor called in except during the epidemic of Spanish flu which in 1919 struck Pincroft in force.

Children on a vitamin deficient diet are prime victims for any virus, and we were mown down like hay before a scythe. Matron, overworked and harassed, brought us hot-water bottles and Bovril as we lay in bed sweating it out. News of the scourge in the world outside was brought to us by the maids mopping the bare lino around our beds. "The flu's spreading all ways," Ethel, cap askew, informed us joyfully, "An 'undred an' twenty-seven deaths in Manchester last week. Worse in Liverpool – they 'ad an 'undred and sixty. More deaths every day that dawns. Like being in t'trenches." This was cheering news for those already feeling like death. But we were encouraged to learn that twenty schools in Birmingham had been closed. We prayed that Pincroft might follow suit. But Miss Sharp remained immune, boosting our morale – even at

[23] Émile Coué – French psychologist/pharmacist, 1857-1926.

the end of February when Ethel announced a grand total of nearly four thousand deaths in the week.

Death, to children, is a meaningless word, something that can never happen to oneself. From that bed-ridden period I remember more clearly the morning Miss Sharp unbelievably gave us each an orange: it was February 27th, and this unprecedented treat was in honour of Princess Pat of Connaught[24] who was that day married to her sailor-lover, Commander the Hon. Alexander Ramsey.[25] Left alone with the news we sucked greedily, spitting out pips to a future generation.

Life returned to normal with the resumption of games. As always, our fullest release from the strictures of Pincroft was on the playing-fields. For one thing we were beyond the orbit of Miss Sharp. And for another, games were pure delight and freedom – even netball had its minor joys. But to play hockey and get into the first eleven meant shrilling matches against all the other schools in Southport and Birkdale who counted players for England among them. Playing centre-half for us was Laura who, at fifteen, became the darling of the coach, Mr Barlow, twenty-five years older. This romance flourished in the heat and mud of practice matches, and later flowered into marriage. Meanwhile it added even more colour to our game. Laura was mercilessly teased by Mildred who was unable to rustle up a future husband among her ever-changing stream of boyfriends, and who was no good at games. It was Laura, tall, dark-haired, athletic, musical, and unacademic, who was the first among us to 'get her man'. She was also, over the horizon, to get three sons and, all too soon, a sick husband and widowhood.

Years later she and I met along with Valerie, the beautiful, green-eyed clergyman's daughter who had foundered over the

[24] Princess Patricia of Connaught (Granddaughter of Queen Victoria) 1886-1974.
[25] Sir Alexander Robert Maule Ramsay, 1881-1972.

Transfiguration, and who had played centre-forward in our team. Memory sheds new light and colour on old friendships and youthful experiences. We recalled our schooldays with delight, considering ourselves fortunate compared with many schoolchildren today who, lacking a framework of discipline, find themselves too often adrift, having no anchor. Pincroft taught us more than Miss Sharp herself realised. The stricter the rules, the stronger the comradeship pulled us together to flout what is unjust. We found ways of making the staff look ridiculous when it suited us. There was the satisfaction of having something against which to rebel. And at school, clustered naturally into groups, we shared each other's triumphs and torments to enjoy a sense of security and belonging I have never experienced since.

To return to school where in reality forbidden fruit was so much enjoyed. As I have said, one of our major pleasures was the delicious talking after 'lights out' about our home lives and our dreams and aspirations. Many were the boasts and exaggerations concerning large country houses, horses, and dogs – not so much cars, owned by very few parents. Mildred, of course, had the most exciting adventures with boyfriends, happily invited by her father, a captain in the Merchant Navy. Laura, who spoke only of brothers and sisters, was rumoured to be adopted – the real daughter of a Russian count. Sometimes our talks expanded to getting out of bed and the indulgence of adolescent curiosity. Someone had observed that Madge, well-developed for her age, had black hair in her armpits. We organised drill, stripped her from the waist, which included raising her arms above her head. When Madge meekly complied we shrieked with delight – to her astonishment. Far more cruel was our inspection of Julia, a senior girl put temporarily in our room. She, it was whispered, was the thrilling sprouter of pubic hairs and full bust – the whole works – which we determined to view. The wretched girl fought vainly to keep her nightie down while three of us pushed aside her clenched hands till she stood uncovered to our hungry gaze. In the absence of full information we gloated over 'juicy' passages in the Bible, speculated on hidden activities, and longed for our flat chests and button nipples to swell out in seductive curves.

Incarcerated at Pincroft, and forbidden newspapers, the drama of Armistice Day, November 11, 1918, that first term, never penetrated. But I remember my mother's joyful face when she took us out on visiting Saturday, and her talk of the end of the war and long, happy years ahead – this while we stuffed ourselves with meringues and trifle in a welter of synthetic cream. We never saw my father at that time. Now acting-colonel, he stayed on in Cairo, studying and still working on cholera. No doubt we suffered at the separation of our parents and from our brave mother's continuous battle against ill-health. Early home life, even under the shadow of a stern father, seemed idyllic, dreamlike when viewed in retrospect from the harsh realities of boarding-school.

Probably my greatest glory at Pincroft was the winning of the gym medal two years running. Third time was for keeps, but Miss Sharp, determined to spike my guns, refused to let me compete because I fainted in church which, of course, had nothing to do with such exercises. Hoping to be an acrobat, I most bitterly resented this interference. Instead of gym practice I was put in charge of the plants in her rooms. Once she challenged me: "Have you watered the aspidistra in my study?" "No, Miss Sharp," I replied. "And why not?" "I'm sorry, Miss Sharp, I forgot." Her cold blue eyes fixed me in a hard stare: "You've no business to forget." The one thing one never gave was a back answer.

Just when I was at the height – in school, games, music, gym, added to the new-found joys of riding on the shore to the pinewoods of Formby, our parents, that is to say, my mother, decided to remove us to Cheltenham College. No doubt Elaine, being so much younger, profited from the move, but I was too deeply entrenched to feel like anything but a plant torn up by the roots. Agony to say goodbye to my friends: I might never see Laura and Valerie again, or ever be uplifted from dark patches by the sardonic remarks of Mildred. As to Elaine, the gulf of three years seemed unbridgeable; we had become strangers.

Chapter 5

Cheltenham Ladies' College

Cheltenham was the blow of my youth, the end of
aspiration.[26] However, on arrival, I felt a lift of the heart
at the sight of the town itself with its white Georgian houses
gilded in autumn sun. The wide streets were bordered with
horse-chestnuts and plane trees far out-shadowing the scrawny
sycamores of Southport. The college, though not architec-
turally beautiful, stretched impressively along a great length of
street, and inside around trim lawns and tidy paths. The acacias
standing sentinel at the cold grey front lodge were orderly and
well-spaced as was everything inside this palace of pitch-pine
and marble, shining with polish and elbow-grease. My class
group, along with several others, was based in the Lower Hall
which had something of a university atmosphere. The even
larger and lighter Princess Hall was used for morning prayers,
special occasions, displays and recitals. Apart from the body of
the hall which held about a thousand, there was also a gallery
running its full length, elegant by contrast to Pincroft's bare
gymnasium.

Here, among eight hundred and thirty-two others, I was
reduced to a mere number, a nonentity known in college only

[26] Cheltenham Ladies' College, founded 1853.

by the colour of my house tie: "Don't swing your arms, Bunwell!"[27] rang in my ears as a prefect,[28] upright, immobile goddess against a pillar, eyed me stonily as I strode rubber-heeled down the Marble Corridor. No speaking was allowed in college without permission from a member of staff, and to enhance this wordless silence all girls wore rubber heels. Great importance was attached to deportment; one must walk with straight back, head upright, swinging one's arms neither too much nor too slightly. In spite of resentful and silent criticism of the school programme, I had to admire many aspects of it. Basic classes of around thirty-five girls were divided into sets of eight or ten for all subjects except English, History and Scripture. Every forty minutes a bell rang 'All Change' and you might have to walk about two miles of corridor, up or down dozens of stairs to get from one room to another.

For a new girl, forbidden to ask the way, this was a nightmare. Driven to enquire rather than miss the class, I was shushed at in horror till one girl whispered: "Ask one of the staff." No comradeship here. And no competition – we were marked as indefinite 'As, Bs and Cs.' Few girls ever achieved A, and if A was the best mark, who really cared whether you had B or C? Yet Cheltenham was a carefully streamed school: 'A' classes were for maths and science; 'B' for English and languages; 'C' for the not quite up to standard. Yet somehow the highly qualified staff seemed to lack the inspiration of those at Pincroft. Not one was a patch on Pincroft's Miss Marks who fired me with enthusiasm to learn more. And Miss Morris, my piano teacher, disapproved of my way of playing; she forbade me ever to play from memory again: "Keep your eyes on the music, never on your hands." By this and other means my photographic memory faded; I was required to plod through every situation. Never a plodder, I sought new

[27] Bunwell House.
[28] Prefect, a pupil who has been given limited authority over other pupils.

directions and aimed at a very bright and amusing girl, also new and in Bunwell House, who sat next to me in class. This was Pat O'Connor, tall, fair, with big china-blue eyes and a squint, daughter of a captain in the Navy. We exchanged written comments on everything, paying scant attention to the lesson in progress. Pat taught me the art of not working while shooting arrows of wit at everyone except our kind form-mistress, Miss Winnington-Ingram, niece of the Bishop of London. Brighter than I, Pat had poor results; she spent hours writing plays and neglecting homework after blank periods in college. Then all at once I discovered Latin – only just begun at Pincroft. After clanging through Caesar's Gallic Wars and alighting on Livy, I came to revel in Ovid's Metamorphoses, reading it as a novel. Towards the end of the summer term we were requested to write a sonnet. To Miss Winnington-Ingram's amazement mine was the only one fit for the college magazine, and I wondered why the best work I was capable of seemed to come with the least effort.

So far I have not mentioned the headmistress because we saw nothing of her except from the platform of the Princess Hall, generally taking prayers. Miss Sparks, who succeeded Miss Faithfull, was to us no more than a figurehead on the prow of a well-manned ship. Short, plump, she daily appeared in her black gown with crimson hood, raised above us, infinitely remote. Yet to judge from her addresses she was kind and sympathetic, if unapproachable. It was equally difficult to get through a bevy of junior goddesses – all tall and beautiful – to the senior games mistress who had no idea of any new girl's capabilities. And this was my biggest grouse of all. About a hundred of us new girls were herded on a windy playing-field, first with hockey and then lacrosse sticks. During the fifteen minutes scramble you were lucky if viewed at all. I hit the hockey ball once and fumbled the lacrosse stick, for me a foreign instrument. I was ordered to spend an entire term 'catching and throwing' in a wearisome exercise I never mastered. Happily, Pat hated all games so together we endured what we had to do, eluded what we could.

Gym was even more disappointing. Never once did we climb the rib-stalls or tackle the horse; parallel bars there were none. For us untried recruits it was drill, drill, drill all the way. Such concentration-camp exercise was alleviated by gazing on the goddess who instructed us; six foot tall with a lithe and wonderful body, this latter-day Diana held us enraptured. Several girls and a small bespectacled maths mistress were in love with her. However, the academic, impersonal, disciplined atmosphere of college allowed little scope for the followers of Sappho. Certainly in our house there was nothing of that. And yet our encounters with the male sex could be described as less than nil. If, for instance, when out on 'crocodile walks' we came in sight of an advancing posse from the boys' college, word flew up from the tail: "Cross to the other side of the road and avert your eyes." Bored with the idea of boys as most of us were, we found this exercise laughable. Indeed, we were far more interested in each other and the staff, though at Cheltenham even 'crushes' were of the mildest. Having grown out of Miss Marks, I found no compensation in the thought of boys, alien creatures, awkward, inarticulate and uncouth. Though many of us may have left college sexually inhibited, I later learned from an Oxford graduate that of all the women up there, those from Cheltenham College behaved the most outrageously.

Real friendships had some chance of flourishing in the more homely atmosphere of life in house. There were forty-two of us at Bunwell where Pat and I sat together at mealtimes, as far removed as possible from the house-mistress, Miss Needler, a degree less stringent than Miss Sharp. She was strict yet, we were told, must be excused a slight acidity of tongue because her fiancé had been killed in the war. All this imparted to us across the tail end of the supper table. "Which war?" Pat had enquired, "the Boer or the Crimea?" Miss Needler had long outgrown her prime.

One day I was summoned to her study and, fearing her displeasure, knocked timidly on the door. Silently she motioned me to sit down. "I want to talk about you and Elaine," she began. "Such an unnatural pair of sisters I've never met. Why, I've never once seen you kissing each other!" She broke off, and I was astounded. Kiss Elaine! – the idea appalled me – it would be too horribly embarrassing, more so for Elaine who would shrink away. I fumbled for words, realising the truth in what she said. Something must have gone wrong in our early days. Were we too much alike in the wrong way or too opposite? Or not quite opposite enough? "Perhaps she doesn't like me," I ventured at last. Perhaps a gap of more than three years was unbridgeable. Maybe she thought me conceited and bossy (unhappily true). A hundred possibilities flitted through my mind. For days after this I tried my best, but was met, as always, by Elaine's averted face. I daren't even tell her what Miss Needler had said.

Caught up in the tide of college life, there was little time for brooding on personal problems, and this one seemed insoluble. As time went on I got into my stride and, resisting temptation from Pat, started to work, mainly because I wanted to leave early. This was easy because everyone worked hard, and good exam results were taken for granted. But there were golden interludes – excursions to lovely Birdlip and Cranham Woods scrambles up Leckhampton Hill, and walking in the town in autumn, through fallen leaves, past the exuberant fountain of prancing horses, and those gracious Georgian houses, gilded with late summer to tea at the Queen's Hotel. There were the Max Mossel concerts and regular visits from the Birmingham Orchestra; there was the theatre; and many celebrities were invited to speak, sing, or play in college. It was there, in the pinewood Princess Hall, that I was awoken to the magic of the spoken word. The day Henry Ainley recited Flecker's Hassan a gate swung open on to undiscovered country.[29]

The summer half-term, 1926, found me slogging through School Certificate exams, having been set back a year by removal from Pincroft. The standard was higher than today's. In what then amounted to 'O' level, for instance, all subjects had to be taken at once. Certain subjects, English, a foreign language, and maths or science were compulsory. Elaine, with eight distinctions, did far better than I, yet because she failed in Latin she failed the whole exam.

Many girls, after taking Higher Schools, went on to take Inter Arts or BSc prior to degree courses. And not long before my time full degrees could be taken at this College which opened in 1853 and was sixteen years ahead of Girton – the Shangri-La of the science girls.[30] What we owed to Dorothea Beale we were never allowed to forget.[31] She was outstanding in her day for courage and single-mindedness in pursuit of higher education for women, and at the age of twenty-seven was appointed College principal. She held this post for forty-eight years running in double harness with Miss Buss of North London Collegiate. Both women were as vital to the life of the college as to each other. A certain inflexibility about Miss Beale was compensated for by the wit and humour of Miss Buss who was affectionately described as 'more than human.' These two, inevitably, were the butt of rhymes and witticisms:

> *Miss Buss and Miss Beale*
> *Cupid's darts do not feel*
> *How different from us*
> *Miss Beale and Miss Buss.*

[29] Henry Ainley – British Shakespearean actor, 1879-1945.
[30] Girton College, established 1869.
[31] Dorothea Beale, Cheltenham College Principal, 1858.

Elaine and Phoebe with their father Dr. Arthur Rayner, 1916.

Phoebe's mother Gertrude Rayner, circa 1916.

Phoebe aged 9 years. Blackpool sands, 1918.

Sullom Holt – Rayner Family 2nd home, 1922.

Cheltenham Ladies College, 1926.
Phoebe aged 17 seated 1st row 4th from right.

Phoebe's father Dr. Arthur Rayner, aged 42.

Phoebe aged 17. Coming out dance 1926.

Phoebe's mother Gertrude aged 50. Coming out dance 1926.

Aubrey and Phoebe Hesketh. Wedding day.
September 30th 1931.

Richard aged 3 yr, Martin aged 6 yr, 1938.

In my day any girl whose behaviour fell short of perfect was bidden to stand in the Marble Corridor, in front of the Beale Memorial, for twenty minutes without moving. This after reading the inscription: 'Of her ideals and achievements this college and the lives she inspired will ever be the true memorial'. In her dedication Miss Beale rivalled the founder of Girton, Emily Davies, whose triumph and courage in flouting Queen Victoria's disapproval of her plan was raised like a flag in our schoolgirl minds. The Queen regarded Girton as one of those "mad, wicked ideas of women's rights." Undeterred, Emily Davies, a rector's daughter, small and stubborn as the Queen herself, had gone ahead and received her first five students at Girton College.

Though Emily determined that her young ladies take the same course as men she also insisted that they behave like ladies. This earned her the approbation of a Cambridge hostess who, after a dinner-party, wrote to a friend of one of them: "My dear, she was a nice girl, with rosy cheeks and nice manners – you wouldn't have thought she knew anything." The Cheltenham hierarchy was imbued with Emily's ideals – that while slogging away at work we should behave with ladylike restraint.

In those days women's university colleges had fewer rules than men's whereas at Cheltenham in the twenties – in spite of the fact that girls mature earlier than boys – we were far more closely hedged against the opposite sex. Consequently there was none of the whispering and giggling about boys as at Pincroft. No secret letters smuggled in and out by day-girls. The emphasis on routine, discipline and the intellect gave me a sense of a world removed from the flesh and the devil. At 6.50 a.m. each day I had a cold bath followed by an hour's practising piano scales in a cold room. Thereafter the day was organised, timed, assessed until the end of prep at 9.30 p.m. And even this was followed by prayers. This regime should

d

have been the best antidote to 'thoughts of love'. Yet Cupid's darts still pierced through, sharper for long seasons in the dark. Spring, with its blossom and birdsong, was a troubling season. Armfuls of daffodils from Cranham Woods, the Evesham cherry orchards, and nightingales, prompted urges of unknown origin. That was the one subject college left in silence and ignorance. I used to lie awake at night listening to a church clock striking every quarter till the first fingers of dawn slipped through the curtains. Sometimes I crept into a neighbour's bed, desperate for comfort and sleep.

As for adolescent lavatory talk and vulgar jokes, there was none of that here. And none of the laughter which had enlivened Pincroft tedium. Indeed, a veil was drawn over all bodily functions till one felt they were regrettable, indecent. A fine-edged mind, surely, could rise above such crudities? Thus I breathed a purer air than of former days. To look back on the reigns of Miss Lofthouse, Miss Sharp and Miss Needler is to understand the inhibitions of children reared under such scratchy wings. I was more than interested to learn yet again, many years later, from a younger friend of mine, headmistress of a well-known school, that at Oxford the girls who most disgraced themselves, staying out late and climbing forbidden garden walls at dawn, were the girls from Cheltenham Ladies' College.

Though the food was better, the houses more comfortable than at Pincroft, the work and discipline were even stiffer. Elaine and I survived both at the cost of certain eccentricities, though Elaine, being more resistant to opposition, emerged better able to deal with awkward people – notably my father – and she was adept at solving tricky problems, simply by letting them wash over her as she continued on her way. We were disappointing daughters in that we refused to attempt the medical careers recommended by my father. Elaine was the college's top violinist and I excelled at nothing but writing sonnets! Anyhow, my academic course was scotched by my mother's advancing ill-health.

Although my father was relieved to have me home for the next few difficult years, he was ahead of his time with regard to women doctors whom he actively encouraged, believing that women have special qualities which in many cases better fit them for the job. No one else seemed to agree with him; women doctors were viewed with suspicion especially by the women themselves. "Don't put your daughter into medicine, Mrs Worthington," was therefore wise advice at a time when women doctors were struggling not only against prejudice, but also the difficulties of running a home with such an exacting career. As for an unmarried woman doctor, she would have sat behind her brass plate waiting in vain for the door-bell.

At the turn of the century it was very difficult for women to become even medical students; not until 1948 were all medical schools co-educational. This meant an eighty per cent intake of men. Then, suddenly, in 1959, came the appointment of the first woman physician to the Queen – Dr Margery Blackie who, like her predecessor, Sir John Weir, was a Fellow of the Faculty of Homeopathy, and consulting physician at the Royal London Homeopathic Hospital. Since this appointment, women doctors have moved several steps up the ladder; and even women patients have overcome their prejudice.

In the twenties it would have been more than unusual for the two daughters of a doctor to become doctors themselves, though not at Cheltenham where we were regarded primarily as 'degree' material. I cannot remember another girl simply 'going home' when she left college. But after twelve years at school, ten of which were boarding, I was fed up with books and rules. My mother's illness gave me a good excuse for returning home without a career in mind – to the dismay of Miss Winnington-Ingram who more than once warned me: "You'll regret it. You ought to try for Oxford." It was easier to get in in those days. But at that moment the call of the wild was stronger than the call of learning.

A deeper reason for this was the feeling of having been cramped overlong emotionally by petty restrictions. Adolescent joys of rebellion were on the wane; besides, at Cheltenham no one seemed to want to rebel. It was such a vast place, and with about twenty houses with their different loyalties, it seemed impossible to find a centre of attachment. And, further, to be penned in a classroom among that lovely, beckoning Cotswold country was almost beyond bearing. I longed to run up the hills, exult in the sun, to be free as the wind.

Chapter 6

A House in the Country

If the most important lesson I learned at Cheltenham was my own unimportance, the first lesson I learned on leaving was that in the world outside there is no freedom. One passes from one pattern of restrictions to another even more difficult, because they must be laid down by oneself. I missed the comforting framework of school routine and discipline. Apart from co-operation with my mother's plans and needs, I had to organise my leisure time. Our ancestors frowned at pleasures hardly earned, but as yet I was too unschooled in life to find pleasure in useful work or helping others. And my mother was too unwell to guide me.

August, 1926, found the four of us on holiday in Llandudno. My mother was cheerful enough during the day and watched us bathe from her deckchair but by evening she began to droop. Blue veins stood out on her fair skin which glistened white as a crocus; and she began to breathe heavily. At these signs my father set out the methylated-spirit burner, pan, and hypodermic syringe. Twenty minutes after her morphine injection she was fine – relaxed and smiling and able to sit at the open window watching the holiday crowds drifting by on the promenade. We tried to brush away that six o'clock shadow, never spoken of between us.

For Elaine and me the chief delight of that holiday was the evening outing to the pier concert. Here I came instantly under the spell of the dashing new conductor, dark-haired, slim and elegant, whose darting movements from the rostrum recalled a dipper on a stone bowing to the river. What a spark of genius. "He's a star!" I whispered rapturously to Elaine who refused to be deflected from the music.

In September Elaine returned to school, and my first whiff of freedom was only faintly marred by my mother's condition, because by now we had a house in the country – the dream of my nursery days in solid fact. In order to explain how this came about, I must turn back to February, 1919 and my father's return from the Middle East. My mother put up flags telling us that he'd been awarded the Order of the British Empire (OBE) for military services as well as research into the prevention of cholera and malaria. His last act as a soldier was to bring home a shipload of men stricken with Spanish flu without a single casualty.

February, 1919, was quite a month – the flu epidemic at its peak; my father restored to our home at No. 9 Ribblesdale Place, and women granted the vote, which news he heard on board ship on his way home. During the Easter holidays, we felt him changing gear, adapting himself once more to the rigours of an indoor, pressurised existence in which he was helped by happy reunions with his loyal workers. We were cheered most of all by my mother's renewed zest which seemed to imply restored health; and by the improvement on the food front. Though many things were scarce, we tasted real butter for the first time in years. And fresh eggs into which we reverently dipped fingers of buttered toast.

During the war no one had taken my father's place in the infirmary X-ray department, but 1919 saw him again in charge aided by his invaluable Sister Slater, dark-eyed, small and neat in her navy dress and shining white cap and apron. In her eighties she recalled those early days for me: "It was fearfully exacting work. No one could guess how much it took out of you. For timing exposures we had to hold a switch, counting the seconds. And your father was a perfectionist: he would have everything just right. But how inspiring to work for," she went on, "Always eager to start and always pleasant. And with the patients he was gentleness itself. I never once knew him lose his temper." When I mentioned his explosiveness at home she smiled, "You'd have understood if you'd realised the nature of the work."

No wonder fireworks shot up from the top of his head when he arrived home exhausted. And my mother, so often disappointed by cancelled plans, hurt and neglected because of his fatigue, did completely understand. "The first lesson you must learn," she would say, "is to accept disappointment." In spite of all, she adored him, respected his dedication, and had the courage to be cheerful in face of his pessimistic nature. Long after they were both dead I read some of their letters which show that he not only depended on her support, but loved her utterly. She was his safety-valve and anchor. And yet unlike him, gay and sociable, she loved parties and entertaining which he so dreaded. As also the formal medical dinners he had to attend, and at which he made witty speeches. Such occasions he said, took the edge off the next day's work: "And I'd much rather work."

People have criticised a way of life in which he put patients first. That this was less than half true is already obvious. Yet on life's workaday level it was true. His meticulous nature was driven mad by our short-comings and repressed needs. Once he called me "a careless little slut" for leaving the top off an ink-bottle. I look back, not with resentment, but with pleasure and pride at his achievements. Having so much to give to so many, he gave it freely. And should three people complain for lack of attention when hundreds in far greater need received so much – often life itself as well as health? It was my mother, far more than us girls, who had to give in and go without.

But before long our lives were to take on a new shape. My mother inherited a considerable sum of money in trust from her wealthy uncle, James Fielding, a Blackburn cotton manufacturer. Suddenly, after years of frustration, disappointment, and skimping, she was within reach of the dream of her life – a house in the country. Early in 1922, overriding my father's objections, she bought Sullom Holt, a white half-timbered, red-roofed house on the slope of Sullom Hill. This lovely place, surrounded by a six-foot beech hedge, with two acres of garden, greenhouses, a model farm, three cottages, and ninety acres of pastureland, was bought for nine thousand pounds.

In initiating this major change in our lives she had taken a brave gamble because my father, while loving the country for walks, never wanted to live there. His work belonged to the town, and so did he. Now he had two houses to maintain, and a ten-mile drive to work and back, including Saturdays and Sundays. While appreciating Sullom, he never ceased to grumble at this when he scrambled up late in the mornings, and arrived back late at night. My mother pointed out that for fifteen years her life had been in subjection to his. At No. 9 we had never known a family life. Friends seldom came; no one ever stayed more than one night because visitors were disruptive of my father's work. And we children had always been hustled out of sight and hearing. Now, at last, we might expand and breathe, invite school-friends home, and even play the piano. We might clatter, uncorrected, up and down the bare oak staircase. There was laughter in the house.

Had my mother realised, she was putting into practice what Aunt Edith and the suffragettes had long fought for. But in

1922 a woman needed more than a vote to assert herself in the face of her husband's work and way of life. She needed money. And now it seemed that my mother was to have a life – far more than a house – of her own. Alas, the removal and upheaval had drained much of her vitality, always of the spirit rather than the body. While encouraging us with music, she never touched her violin, now being played by Elaine. Yet unsparing of strength, she worked continuously in the house and garden till everywhere flowered and shone. Underneath every effort lay the determination that my father should come to love the place and, indeed, on fine Sunday afternoons walking up the hill behind the house he would exclaim in delight at the view of sea and mountains. Often it seemed that her plan to include him in our pleasure was fully justified. As for us, it was paradise after No. 9, the park, and town pavements. Friends came for lunch and tea, seldom for dinner – a meal sacred to my father; there were tennis-parties, picnics and walks over the fells.

In spite of all, my father never quite belonged. And after his day's work he seemed further apart from us than ever. Every device was used to restore him: the moment the car scrunched to a stop my mother would open the door in greeting while we scuttled like rabbits into the background. "I'm jiggered up!" he would say taking off his hat and coat while Whewell, the chauffeur, crept in silently with his bag of works. In the drawing-room sherry glasses winked in the firelight. We sat silent while he sipped, and my mother quietly left the room to placate the cook who would grumble at overdone meals.

Dinner was a silent meal except for the gently fizzing cider which my father loved. Not until he attacked the cheese with his vigorous knife, and butter sparingly scraped on and off a water-biscuit was there an easing of tension, but still no talk. Back again in front of the fire he would light his beloved cigar – Ramón Allones – unfold the *Lancashire Daily Post*, and undo a waistcoat button.[32] At last he was relaxed and we could breathe. Even so, we never spoke unless, rarely, he made a remark. At half-past ten the parlour-maid brought in his whisky and soda; it was my job to pour out his 'two fingers only'– as instructed every night. While he sipped, my mother at last might speak to him of urgent matters. She never troubled him with purely domestic problems. Occasionally he would expand so much as to ask for a gramophone record of John Coates, John McCormack or Walter Glyn singing one of his favourite tenor songs. These tuneful Victorian melodies would carry him away to a rosy world of romance and 'might-have-been' beyond the grinding responsibilities of his work. Woe unto us if during this interlude the telephone should ring. One of us would hasten to silence it, imploring for a message which we might tactfully convey so as to avoid repercussions. By now there was a growing private practice of neighbours, mostly wealthy landowners and country gentry. One of these, a querulous old millionaire, forever concerned for his health, was a regular telephone offender. "Damn and blast!" my father would explode, carefully cradling his cigar before getting up. Then from the hall came the dulcet tones of his 'telephone' voice. If the caller were a woman the tone was even more courteous and reassuring. But when fellow doctors called him in consultation on worrying cases he was instantly alert to go out. Among these were two doctors in partnership who rejoiced in the names of Patchett and Matchett.

On the whole his patients were well-trained not to ring at inopportune moments and never, unless urgent, during the night. Perhaps the call we most dreaded was during or just after Sunday lunch which, because my father did his private round after the infirmary on Sundays, never started till two o'clock at the earliest. I remember one summer Sunday when the telephone shrilled above the roast beef. It was one of my

[32] Ramón Allones Cuban cigar.

friends on a trivial matter. "Tell her," he said on my return to the table, "that anyone who rings up at two o'clock on a Sunday ought to be shot."

Notwithstanding the problems which seemed to gather weight with time, he found some pleasure in our new house, viewing birds through field-glasses, amassing names of wild flowers, and even attempting a limited form of gardening. On fine Sundays he'd spend a happy hour on the lawns rooting up daisies with a two-pronged fork. "Like rooting out a cancer," I teased him. And he became the man he really was.

He left social life to my mother who was disappointed to find his dislike of parties reflected in me. But unlike him I made no effort to be pleasant to other people unless I knew them well. Even so, soon after I left school my mother made one last attempt on my behalf. Dismayed by my lack of interest in the 'spotty sex', she insisted on giving me a coming-out dance which, fashionable then, would today seem as absurd to everyone as at the time it did to me. A robust nine stone, I had to be stuffed unwillingly into white taffeta bordered with pink roses. My poor mother worked so hard at such unyielding material – I even objected that the dress made me look fatter than usual – and sent out a hundred and fifty invitations for this affair to be held at Preston's Bull and Royal hotel. There were banks of flowers, champagne, a good band and supper. Yet on the afternoon of the dance I flung myself on my bed and sulked. Nine o'clock found me stationed by a pillar, pink and white programme and pencil in hand, waiting for partners. Of course I knew that none of the young men wanted to dance with me, but they were bound to come up and ask: "May I have the pleasure of number six or nine?" as the case might be, after which they turned away. No one asked me for more than one dance except my father whose enthusiasm was as faint as mine. But at least he put on a smile with white kid gloves and gave the appearance of enjoyment, while I struggled through the performance longing for two o'clock to come. That night it was my mother who triumphed. With her golden hair and dress of gold lace over old rose she looked radiant, waltzing her way through the hours, light-foot, light-heart as a girl of twenty, attracting all the men who hastened from my side.

Chapter 7

Gathering Shadows

It was the last day of spring, 1927. Aged 18 years, I lived at home while Elaine was still at school. My mother was unable to walk with me or do more in the garden than 'dead head' the roses. Only six months ago she had been a whirl of gold-and-pink gaiety. Still beautiful, but fast fading, she sat outside on June 20th 1927, her fifty-first birthday. Never complaining, she revelled in every moment as though this, indeed, would be her last summer. Each rose snipped off seemed symbolical of her life. With a basketful of dead heads she sat down exhausted on the uncomfortable iron garden seat. As she closed her eyes and smiled into the sun I felt a shameful flicker of irritation: why couldn't she be well for this my first year of freedom? Oh, the selfish intolerance of youth trying to grab all with both hands, taking, taking, and giving so little in return. Yet dark in the background lurked the clubfoot shadow of fear. I was peering into an abyss. All around was the colour and shimmer of approaching summer in her garden, yet happiness refused to be born.

My mother now had a companion-help, Miss Fender, who was a little help and a huge snob only coming to life when a 'title' took the telephone. "Lord Mountmorris," she announced one evening, flushed with pleasure, "would like a word with the doctor." Unhappily at this time my father was unable to give my mother the attention she needed. More pressing than private patients were the many court cases, requiring days away, in which he became involved. He was for ever being called to give evidence in workmen's compensation cases. Dr Simpson, a loyal friend, expanded to me on this activity: "He was often in competition with his own colleagues – Dr McKerrow for one, a brilliant surgeon who generally knew a great deal more about the case but had no idea of presenting it. Your father's presentation and timing were masterly. He was clear, firm, eloquent, persuasive, and often won a case which should have gone the other way." Years later I was asked by a well known judge if I were Dr Rayner's daughter. How delighted I was at his reply: "Your father was the best medical witness I knew. Never ruffled and however much they tried to trip him up and tie him in knots, he stuck to the point."

For all his grumbles that this work, demanding hours, days of overtime, interfered with his routine, my father obviously enjoyed the drama of the court-room. Enjoyed too, examining the patient. One of these, a builder's mate from Blackpool, came for examination after a fall from scaffolding. Every inch was carefully explored; many questions were asked. "Well, doctor," the man remarked as he put on his jacket, "I mun thank 'ee very much. Thou'st treated me very well." Surprised, my father enquired, "And how did you expect me to treat you?" "Nay, doctor," the man replied, "thou doesn't know t'name thou'st got. When mi mate 'eard as I was coming ter thee, 'e said: Art a going ter that little bugger from Preston? Then it's God 'elp thee."

Since the move to Sullom Holt, his work was conducted at No. 29, Ribblesdale Place, opposite No. 9 on the dull side of the street, whose houses had no gardens, no view of the park. Though still large, they were considerably cheaper. It was in the X-ray/Consulting room that I came to know my father as a man more fulfilled at work than at home or on holiday. In his company I felt at peace, 'in harbour' in spite of his occasional fireworks.

Just now my mother's condition prevented her from being the safety-valve he so badly needed. On the contrary, instead of letting off steam as in the earlier years, he spoke gently, tenderly to her – not because he had come to love her any more but because he understood her need for comfort. His outbursts were reserved for me and Whewell, his devoted and more than long-suffering chauffeur. Very occasionally he managed to take a Saturday afternoon off to take my mother for a drive. This was surely an ominous sign. One Saturday he called in two well-known surgeons from Leeds and Manchester. The three of them spent ages upstairs and even longer downstairs, discussing my mother's condition. It was decided that she should have an exploratory operation. A month later she was home again, much depleted and needing a nurse, with me to fill in off-duty hours.

Now I had to act as buffer between bedroom and kitchen. With the maids resenting the nurse, I had much ado to keep the peace. Meanwhile, my father did night-duty every night and so began the regime of bed-pans, blanket-baths, and the eternal traffic of trays. At first, hoping for her recovery, I managed to cope, however inexpertly. But there was no improvement; she was often in pain, and I began to find her brave smile unbearable. The nurse gave neither moral support nor encouragement, and my father, arriving home tired and worried at night, needed both. By now, my mother was having regular morphine injections and in her weak state refused to let nurse give them. "She's so rough; she stabs me," she moaned. So my father taught me how to pinch up the skin of her arm into a bulge and insert the needle swift and slantwise. My mother cheered me by saying she never felt it. But she couldn't wait for the next dose which I never dreamed of giving before the appointed time, in spite of moans and entreaties.

In contrast to morphine was her craving for moss. Someone had sent her a plant bedded in moss whose strong, damp, earthy smell gave her more pleasure than any flowers. It captured for her the out-of-reach woods and fields. So Elaine and I used to hunt alongside streams and ditches pulling out wads of the dark velvet-green stuff which we placed on saucers by her bedside. When we brought in a fresh supply she would ask us to hold it under her nose so that she could breathe it deep, deep into her lungs. One morning, though she was weaker every day, my father took her to the Infirmary for a massive X-ray. All that day the whole department was shut down to other patients. A few days after this, I learned that she had to undergo a major operation.

This was the month of September. During her three-week absence I almost forgot the sickroom smell in galloping my pony over the moors and the glory of being young. Vaguely I remember her return and the seeming improvement so soon to be swamped again in tides of pain and discomfort. Now she had both a day and a night nurse, and my father moved into the spare room except for nurse's off-duty nights. I knew now that she had cancer; a three-inch length of gut had been removed from the colon: "It was a marvellous plumbing job," my father told me, "but goodness knows what's to come." We kept the hateful secret, telling her she had colitis, but what came was a secondary cancer of the liver. Now I had two nurses and fortunately there was a Nurse Griffiths, kind and easy, who slotted beautifully into our lives and taught me to play Bezique during the long sickroom vigils. To have us both near helped my mother to endure a little longer before the next injection.

When nurse had gone off duty she would have me curl up on the wide window-ledge watching for the headlights of my father's car as it swept down the hill a mile away. He always gave her the last injection of the day and this waiting period was torment. Worn down with pain and weakness she would cry out for an hour and more: "The lights! The lights! Are they coming? Oh, make them come!" Distressed and helpless, I held her hand, a fragile bunch of bones in a bag of flesh. With her ivory-yellow sunken cheeks, she was little more than a skeleton. And in spite of treating her heels and buttocks with meths, powder and such-like, bed-sores were developing. Her lovely matt blue eyes become opaque pupils pin-pointed with morphine, the bright corn-coloured hair reduced to a mousy wisp. She, once my champion, support and source of encouragement, lay there at my mercy pleading for relief and release from pain. I was too young, too disciplined in obedience, to give what she longed for. Instead, anger and resentment at this hideous disease smouldered in me, and sometimes flared, alas, in thoughtless or unkind words. Inexplicably the distress I felt on her account thus added to her sum of misery. Immature and bewildered, I felt like a dream figure moving outside a fearful charade – here was something too horrible for involvement. Stumbling to the lavatory to empty the bed-pan after a severe haemorrhage, I was sometimes sick over the contents.

For respite I plunged more ardently into the delights of walking and riding in the bracken-and-heather smell of the moors and, for blessed intervals, forgetting the pain and weariness in wait. That autumn, in contrast with the sickroom, the woods were alight with fox-red beeches, yellow poplars and nutmeg-coloured oaks, the whole earth aromatic in rich decay. Full of health, vitality and the glory of movement uphill and down, I explored the countryside bathed in sun. October, with misty breath and silver dews and frosts, merged into November – still alive and full of colour. At this time of year a feeling of expectancy swells through the shortening days before Christmas. Yet so often now, as I swung downhill from the stables, I could hear my mother screaming with pain through the open window. My father must have been over-scrupulous with the morphine, though one morning, vigorously dissolving the quarter-grain, he said under his breath: "No one dies of cancer these days. They die of morphine poisoning." Looking back, I understand that he was torn between the desire to relieve pain and the fear of killing. What I cannot understand is that never, even during my mother's worst agonies, did it occur to me to give her a bigger dose. Now, in later life, I could never withstand those endlessly repeated cries: "Give it me! Give it me!" And every evening: "The lights, the lights! Make them come!"

In spite of this my mother was no weakling; she battled on, clinging to a cobweb strand of hope. Until one day when she lay moaning with pain in her back, the new, beautiful, hard-faced Irish nurse snapped at her: "What can you expect with cancer of the liver?" A sudden, tense silence filled the room. Then I learned what is meant by 'turning your face to the wall'. My mother had given up all hope and longed to die. I was filled with guilt at being alive and ashamed at every service we provided for her. She no longer smiled in rare intervals of peace and swallowed mouthfuls of liquid food like a prison victim. In truth, she had become our victim; a woman in the condemned cell. All that mattered now was the injection.

January and my nineteenth birthday came in cold and hard, followed by a dragging wet February. My father said, "Such typical English weather with grey, dull, sullen skies and not a gleam of light." That summed up life for us. This same month last year my mother's youngest sister, Mab had been carried off by an unidentifiable virus. There were no medications to rescue her in those days. The day of the funeral had seen February at its harshest with sleet driven by a whiplash wind. Though my father begged my mother, shadowy as a ghost, not to go, she had insisted on getting up from bed to attend the service. Afterwards she stood by the graveside where the sleet, thickening to snow, whitened the collar of her brown fur coat. Maybe the shock and sorrow of her loved sister's death, more than the weather, accelerated her decline. From that day it was downhill all the way.

"It's a bad business," my father shook his head. "The two sisters on the same hillside, both marked down in early middle-age." His was a Hardyesque view of fate as a dark shadow in the background, waiting to reach out a hand with every going down of the sun. "In the end," he said, "we can do nothing except relieve pain and discomfort. God knows what it's all about."

Neither he nor my mother had ever talked about death in front of me. And now I had no wish to discuss a subject far too distant, so it seemed, to be a personal threat. Death was an outsider. I remember looking at those hundreds of wreaths snow-fingered on my aunt's grave, and thinking: "What a waste." Youth, resilient and selfish, recovers from such losses and tragedies with heartless ease. Heartless myself, I swept the subject under the carpet. Yet I suffered from a feeling of familiar landmarks slipping away, and the need for a raft to cling to. The one raft in that stormy sea was my father. More than that, he was a roof over my head and world.

To return to February, 1928, and my mother almost transparent with disease; nights and days merged in sickroom routine, relieved only by riding and my father's presence in the evenings. We moved as automatons; friends and relatives came and went like shadows. Yet in spite of her illness my mother was still concerned about my lack of social life in contrast with the 'suitable' young men who flocked around my cousin Enid with her long red hair. Hoping I might meet someone, she encouraged me to go out with the Oakenclough Beagles which hunted nearby. Though not interested in the hunting, I loved the exhilarating runs over moorland and heather. But except for one or two youths who briefly appeared, then disappeared to University, the young rural males seemed to be mostly inarticulate and quite unable to sustain a conversation. I wondered how they ever got around to asking anyone to marry them. How I dreaded those invitations to dances on a country estate where hundreds of pheasants were reared in coops for shooting. The sight and sound of those men with guns setting out in pursuit of half-tame, hand-fed birds, almost too heavy to fly, revolted me. The only man with whom I had any meaningful conversation, at this time, was described by them as 'wet'. Both loners at a hunt ball, we drifted together under a potted palm and talked away the remaining dances. He was later to become a high court judge.

Then there were the occasional officers who came for exercise from Fulwood Barracks, ever ready for meals, drinks and surface chats. The truth was, I did not like young men. And just now with my father's irritability increasing under the strain of home life, matrimony seemed a fearful hazard. If I were ever to enter the bonds, I told myself, it must be with someone of even temper who kept regular hours – no doctors for me. And no soldiers either.

March, in the grip of frost and snow, was slowly melting into April. Once again the birds were singing and hedgerows were springing green. Primroses and anemones appeared in the banks, and the rock-garden was a miracle of shining yellows, blues, pinks and purples, while the smell of wallflowers drifted in through windows. The entire world was young and gay except for my mother. Going into her room was like passing from life into death. Masses of flowers arrived: great bunches of roses and carnations; lilies-of-the-valley from a summer never to be reached – fragrant, tantalising symbols of hope and promise, they seemed cruelly out of place beside the shrinking figure in the bed. Day by day the pain grew more intense with that other obscene flower expanding in her entrails. Weakened by the fierce onslaughts, she spoke little, moaning continuously like a wounded pigeon. The saucers of moss brought only a flicker of gratitude while the doses of morphine – though increased – remained minimal by today's standards.

One long-drawn-out suffering evening while we waited anxiously for my father's headlights, a tawny owl cried loud and clear as an oboe out of the darkness. "He's calling me! Listen." The words were only just audible. And that night my father was later than he'd been for months. Hours went by before his arrival, the delayed injection, and merciful sleep. Oh, I thought later, lying in bed, why does she have to wake up? I had begun to long for her to die. Whether it was the morphine or the disease that finally carried her away, she crossed the hairbreadth border on the evening of April 23rd, St George's Day, also chosen for death by Shakespeare and Wordsworth. At last she was rid of the dragon pain.

Chapter 8

New Life After the Funeral

After my mother's funeral in May 1928, my father took Elaine and me for a holiday in the Lake District. We stayed at Castlerigg Manor, near Keswick, where my father, an expert mountaineer, had full scope for his abilities in climbing Scafell by Piers Ghyll, and hauling us beginners up Broadstand. Trim and handsome, at forty-nine he looked years younger, and he plunged into work with renewed vigour. Far more than social life, work was his balm and restorative, the surest bulwark against grief. In this he both lost and found himself. After long hard days, he would return home exhausted but gladly drive off each morning to the place in which he belonged. No one but his faithful Middlehurst and the infirmary sisters could have realised the depth of his giving. As for me, standing in for my mother, I had no idea of it. Half looking forward to, half dreading his return, I used to open the door and greet him as she had done, ready for the frequent reply: "I'm jiggered up." Whereupon Whewell, following dog-like with his black bag, relieved him of his hat and coat. No nurses now, and no anguished mother, the house seemed dead until he came home. However tired he might be, the moment he stepped over the threshold the house came to life, albeit uncomfortable life.

Cooks came and went and none of them suffered gladly his late hours. While they glowered over overdone beef in the kitchen, he slowly sipped his sherry rightly refusing to eat on the instant of return. On one occasion, arriving home later and crosser than usual, he halted on the rug alongside the inner hall door, and sniffed: "My God, what the devil is this foul and filthy stench?" I replied, "It's onions, Daddy," faltering as the strong smell drifted through. "Onions!" he thundered. "I'll never have another onion grown in this garden." Though in awe of him, I knew that such storms meant nothing, and that under the fireworks was a deep well of comfort.

By now the X-ray and Light department was busier than ever and received patients in hundreds at a centre whose equipment was among the best in the country. Yet in the early twenties there were no blood transfusions. In 1922, with the newly-discovered insulin saving the lives of thousands, many primitive methods were still in use. Such as 'cupping' which meant covering boils and swellings with a hot cup to draw out the poison. And even leeches were used – an ancient practice which has been revived today. Before salvarsan to combat syphilis, out came the mosquitoes with the idea of raising the temperature by causing malaria. It was indeed a hit-and-miss treatment. These medieval practices went on in leading London hospitals as well as in the provinces. Preston had not won its high reputation for nothing; the medical as well as the X-ray department remained in the forefront for new treatments and drugs which my father found of absorbing interest.

According to one of his nursing sisters, human interests were not neglected. During a spell of severe winter weather when unavoidably delayed, he sometimes turned up in riding-kit having walked through the snow carrying paraffin, bread, and other necessities to patients half-buried in farms and cottages. One evening, working late with his nursing sister, she challenged him: "I think you are wonderful, but heaven preserve me from marrying a doctor!" He was silent, and she went on, "A doctor's wife must have a terrible time – irregular meals, broken engagements, a lifetime of waiting and playing second fiddle." If only she knew how right she was.

Work continued to come in from all parts of the country, one couple travelling from Penzance to be cured of an obstinate skin disease. More and more court cases piled up, yet the extra load was cheerfully bourne by Middlehurst who was by now virtually a partner in the firm.

At this time my father was getting attention from other devotees than nurses. Often the telephone summoned him to the side of some not-so-old widow or spinster with little of a medical nature to complain of. One of these ladies combined persistence with attractiveness and capability. "Emma is such a clever girl; she'd make your father an admirable wife. Do ask her to tea," suggested a thoughtful aunt. "And think how it would free you to go away." This was a consideration, and I broke through my father's Sunday guest barrier by asking her, many times, to tea. She was the sort of person who did everything well without making you feel inferior, and gave me hints on housekeeping and gardening which made these processes, so painful to me, seem almost enjoyable. My father admired her smartness and sparkling conversation. Yet though he often visited her, and she drank many cups of tea with us, the relationship made no progress. "Emma has such long, narrow feet," he remarked one day. "I could never live with them. Besides, she talks too much."

It was during this period that I met my future husband, Aubrey Hesketh, of the family firm T. M. Hesketh and Sons, cotton-spinners, Bolton, Lancashire. I first saw him being led in as winner of the Pendle Forest Adjacent Hunts Steeplechase, and from that moment was determined to have him. I fell in love with him and married him in spite of my father's gloomy views on the subject. "After long observation I've come to believe that fifty per cent of married couples rub along and make the best of it, forty-five per cent hate one another like poison, and five per cent are really happy."

Ignoring my father's views on marriage and wrapped in rosy dreams, I had not so far considered the implications of marriage itself till one day I sat down with the prayer book and read through the service. I was appalled by those tremendous vows, the everlastingness of such a bond between two imperfect mortals, and the inexorable, unbreakable promises in face of growing older and different – even apart – till such bonds might tighten into bondage. "Let's get married in a registry office," I suggested. Aubrey, with his straightforward, uncomplicated nature, was baffled. If you wanted to be married you were married in church. Only actors, gypsies, and criminals went their own way. I voiced my reservations to both families. Saying little they said all with faintly shocked expressions, I had no choice but to give in and we were married in 1931.

So absorbed was I in my own happiness and the birth of two boys, I had no thought for my father's. When Elaine, now housekeeping for him, told me that more than once he had invited a young girl, younger than herself, to the hallowed Sunday tea, I took no heed. It never occurred to me that he must be very lonely with no one at the centre of his life. It seemed that May, as this new visitor was called, worked at the Victorian cafe where my father went every day for lunch. He was then approaching sixty while she was in her early twenties. The following winter, fate provided ideal conditions for a budding romance. While snowballing on the flat roof of the cafe, May fell and broke her pelvis in three places – an accident leading to three months in hospital, many X-rays, and my father's devoted attention. In spite of his sternly realistic views, a strong romantic vein ran beneath the scepticism: tenderness and chivalry oddly at variance with the steely barbs we knew so well.

e

Born in December, a true Sagittarian, my father the Archer now exchanged his arrow for a sword, becoming knight to his fair lady. In these roles they were admirably suited – protector and protected, each fulfilling a need in the other. Perhaps unconsciously he had chosen someone who would never want to entertain socially. With Emma he would have had to endure sparkling dinner-parties (wheedled into a dinner jacket, God forbid) and the dreaded tedium of polite conversation. Whereas with May he would be free to live simply, untroubled by social demands.

I had not considered this when one day Elaine told me that they were to be married. I'd not even met May, and the idea of one's father marrying someone younger than his daughters seemed outrageous, impossible. Children, while seeking their own happiness, are markedly intolerant of their parents' second choices. I was so overcome by this news, never breathed to me by my father himself, that one day, foolishly and unadvisedly, I went over to his rooms to voice my dismay: "I can't see it leading to happiness." He looked at me with eyes like blue stones and very properly told me to get out.

They were married on the last day of May, 1939, May's twenty-third birthday. May and December in all ways, yet a snapshot from their Llandudno honeymoon shows him jaunty and full of verve as 'The Man who broke the Bank at Monte Carlo'. Together they rambled about the countryside, recited poetry, and seemed ideally happy. Back home the business of running Sullom and coping with maids was another matter. Used to the close ties of family life May felt lost and lonely – especially since Elaine had joined the WRNS.[33] But she put all her energy, pride and polish into those shining oak floors and silver hinges. Now more than ever it seemed pointless to keep up a big place in the country where neither of them belonged.

[33] Women's Royal Naval Service. Women sailors are still known as 'Wrens' or 'Jennies'.

After seven years my father sold up, exchanging this lovely, demanding house for a little red-brick villa in Fulwood, a suburb of Preston. From the Box, as we called it, May was within reach of her family; my father of his work where they were both at home.

Marriage or no, work continued unabated, and though he showed more consideration for May's contentment than he had for my mother's, arriving home at eight instead of nine o'clock in the evening, she too, often felt left out in face of his 'first love'. In spite of all, they had much to give one another: for him someone who cared, someone to return to at the end of the day. And for her the full store of his mind to feed upon. In his early sixties he seemed younger than ever. A young wife and a new house meant new life for him. He had even broken his long habit, so deplored by my mother, of breakfasting in his dressing gown. My relationship with him continued at a deeper level – through letters. Another link was the old enemy telephone. If I left too long a gap he would accuse me: "Well, and what have you been up to? It's a long time since I heard from you." With his telephone allergy he never rang himself.

Perhaps he could express his true feelings only on paper and at a distance. Recalling our family life together, he writes:

As I think of my marriage with your mother and our early life together. It all seems like yesterday. I often regret I didn't value it more when I had it, didn't clutch and hold it realising it was fast passing and wasn't given me forever. It is strange how we are apt to think and behave, in respect of those who are nearest to us, as if everything were permanent, and our present life couldn't change, but that some future plan were more pressing and more important. Then one day we wake up to find the bottom of our world has fallen out. Too late we realise that we had never really been conscious of what we had enjoyed – in such vain, imaginary security. When I go up to my quiet room at night with its pool of light shed by my bedside-lamp encircled by a veil of shadow, I always think of your mother, and of you and Elaine and our life together.

Loyalty to the past was equalled by loyalty to the present. In the same letter he writes of May's care and companionship, and more – the essential part she plays in his life now. *'I well realise how much she gives me.'* And this much he often enlarged upon as the years went by with understanding and affection growing between them. A second wife, in the nature of things, not only marries the man; she marries his memories. He wrote to me as he did from a sense of divided loyalties, anxious to assure me that this new marriage in no way cancelled out the first. In fact, both fulfilled his destiny, and in some strange way became one. While his first wife bore his children and experienced the difficulties, irritations, and joys of earlier years, the second, reaping the mellowness of harvest, was to endure the slow decline into age, illness and death. Both suffered from isolation and loneliness in the face of his work, and both found rewarding happiness in his presence.

Chapter 9

Marriage, Birth of Martin and Richard

Happily my father took an instant liking, as everyone did, to my husband Aubrey whose giving, congenial nature seemed to make everyone his friend. Always responsive to the views of others, he never touched my father on the raw: "Yes yes, I quite agree doctor," he would reply to many a contentious statement, often relating to the iniquities of left-wingers. They couldn't have differed more in temperament; my father's acerbity and sharp wit, cushioned by Aubrey's mildness and affability.

Following our marriage in 1931, we lived in the hamlet of Rivington, in Fisher House, a lovely damp, draughty Georgian house whose white front glimmered behind the trees which surrounded it. For the first five years we survived without electricity or water laid on, (no fridge, washing machine or vacuum cleaner).

Every Sunday, we drove over to Sullom Holt for lunch. At that time Elaine, in charge of the household was often away on courses. She had diplomas in horticulture and ballet dancing, and The Institute of the Horse, which led her in to being a first class riding instructor. Not only this, she became a VAD[34] working in a hospital, and following her winning of the Greenop Medal for the violin at Cheltenham Ladies' College, joined an orchestra, taking the violin as a second subject. Eventually, after serving in the WRNS, she qualified as a full time teacher in secondary schools. "She must be the most highly trained woman in England," remarked my father. "And to crown all," I added to Aubrey later, "she's the only one who can manage him!"

And yet, after gaining eight distinctions in the School Certificate exam, she failed the whole because she failed in Latin. Strange that such a 'failure' should teach French to the Russell children, sons of the Duke of Bedford, and related to Bertram Russell. While my younger sister was gaining knowledge and skills, I was contentedly darning socks and making apple pies. Hearing of my pleasure in such newly discovered marital activities, my father remarked: "That sort of feeling lasts about six months!"

A much greater pleasure was in the world of horses and hunting to which Aubrey introduced me. From nursery days, as already implied, I was mad about horses – a condition enjoyed by all the Hesketh family. My father-in-law, besides his own three or four, kept many of his friends' horses till there were as many as ten or eleven to be stabled. This as well as kennels – he had a passion for bull terriers which he bred and showed. Racing pigeons became almost an obsession; on the night of Aubrey's birth my father-in-law sat up, waiting not his son's arrival, but the return of a prize bird.

Shorefield, the Hesketh house, was always full, mostly of hunting folk and country lovers. No one was turned away from the ample table; no bed remained empty for long. Table talk, naturally revolved around horses, dogs and details of good

[34] VAD, Voluntary Aid Detachment: Founded 1909. Voluntary Unit providing nursing services.

runs, falls, victories at race meetings and in the show ring. For a time, I was entranced by this strange and colourful new world, overjoyed when offered their chestnut mare, Tango, for hunting whenever I wished, and I wished for nothing more at the time.

Then one day came Clement Henniker-Heaton, an ardent follower not only of hounds, but of Betty, Aubrey's younger sister – a true Diana who rode in one of the country's first women's point-to-point steeplechases. I realised, at once, that Clement was different; he was intellectual – as opposed to an intellectual. Though he loved hunting, he made conversation suddenly interesting. Whereas my father-in-law would sweep aside with a laugh any remark that seemed to invite thought, Clement was a natural thinker and observer, and I was disappointed when none of his opening remarks was given air. In spite of exhilarating days in the saddle, and vibrant health, I began to feel there was something missing in this brave new life. Amid such kindness and hospitality, I felt guilty for not being wholly grateful for everything around me.

Aubrey, a naturally happy man, was content in his accustomed pursuits: working in the family firm, having lunch every day at home with the family, and back every evening at six o'clock to his new home with me. Though Bolton-le-Moors, as it is properly named, was indeed surrounded by moors, they were grubby and drab from dark plumes of smoke from mill chimneys. And how apt that the walls over which we leapt while hunting were made of millstone grit. I longed for the cleaner softer countryside I had left, missed the taller fuller trees, abundant wild flowers, and birds in their true colours. As time went by I missed, more and more, talk about ideas, books and the arts. This may sound priggish but there's a shallowness and aridity in talk confined to country sports. I love the country, not merely for the hunting and fishing and other pursuits it provides, but for itself. My greatest joy had been long, often solitary, walks following rivers or climbing hills with my mind still, or wandering according to mood.

The Hesketh family were all active, energetic and high-spirited with the possible exception of Betty's twin, John, the only one who read, who sometimes withdrew into himself, and quite often, mysteriously disappeared from the house. "Brother John's our will-o'-the-wisp – a one on his own," they would say. And he was the only one to do well at school, would have done well at university, had his father not taken for granted that he would go into the mill. No sooner had he left Marlborough school than he found himself in the office of the family business – T.M.Hesketh and Sons. All three brothers went to public schools as was the custom in those days for upper middle class families. Tommy, the second son, did win a prize at Malvern, but Charterhouse was wasted on Aubrey whose true gifts – of the spirit rather than the mind – such as music were never developed.

In fact music, love of the country and horses were what we shared; and all too few days spent walking in the country were what I most enjoyed. Gradually, such days became rarer; Aubrey, public-spirited, and ever ready to oblige was roped in for many committees and public duties. Being chairman of the village school governors, the parish council, the parochial church council, on the committee of various charities and agricultural shows, swallowed many evenings, apart from those at the drill hall with his fellows in the Duke of Lancaster's Own Yeomanry. And, friend of his spinners, who loved and respected him, he attended nearly all their social evenings, hot-pot suppers, bowling matches, and dances. To these last I, too, would have gone, but rarely did so – on his insistence that I must go only if I wanted to. As I didn't want to, and knew he could only spare me the first and last dance, I let him go alone, knowing he would more enjoy the evening. This was a mistake I have since regretted.

Added to these activities were the occasional 'social' dinners which bored me because again, there was rarely any 'interesting talk' (what a prig I was!). Our guests and hosts were generally well-off people from the textile industry or the hunting field. In those days, the women still retired after dinner to the drawing room while the men settled to their own interests over the port. How I wished I could join them – away from idle gossip and the cost of food.

In August 1932, our first son Martin was born. Dismayed at being pregnant a year after marriage, I continued not only riding, but galloping up and down the moors, hoping that I may have at least another year of freedom. The 'gentle trotting' suggested by the doctor, developed into thrilling races with a friend up the steep rough road to Belmont, and back to Rivington till our ponies were in a lather. But the baby was there to stay. It was a horrid birth, partly owing to my doctor's partiality to whisky which he and my father drank downstairs while I was upstairs in the last throes of labour. Not until this performance had continued for twenty-one hours did the midwife report that the baby was the wrong way up. In fact he was lying sideways. An anaesthetist was hastily summoned and the baby removed, blue-faced and barely alive. Of this stage I remember nothing, not even the remark to my shocked mother-in-law who was apparently sympathising with me about the bad time I'd had. Afterwards Aubrey told me that I'd fervently responded with "It was absolutely bloody!" This word, at that time, was never uttered by 'respectable' women.

Perhaps this was the start of my love-hate relationship with men – and God. A man had made me pregnant; a man had made a woeful mess of delivery which resulted in a horrendous repair operation so that in the course of having three children and accompanied by complicated repairs, I was opened and sewn up five times.

The years from 1932-1935 were uncomfortable, not only

physically and sexually but emotionally. When the baby – a real rosy beauty with golden curls – had actually landed, I was both thrilled and proud. But I was not naturally maternal and worried over the least pimple and cold, faithfully following Trudy Kings' methods of regular feeding and potting. I was a superb cow, but sternly refused to breast-feed between 11 p.m. and 6 a.m. with the resulting broken nights.

The years passed and I spent all my spare time riding and hunting with the Holcombe Harriers. As I mentioned, riding and listening to music were the two enjoyments Aubrey and I shared. But on the hunting field, as on the dance floor, I rarely saw him. He was off on his own, following a line, and raising his bowler hat for Master and huntsmen to follow. His job it was to pacify the farmers over whose fields we so joyfully galloped. In truth he should have been a farmer and never boxed up in the offices of mills to become a director of T.M. Hesketh and Sons. Later he bore the burdens and shared the disaster of the shrinking textile industry.

By the spring of 1935 I was again pregnant, and still riding. This birth, except for the actual excruciatingly painful arrival, was a happy experience. Though due at the end of November, the boy, in advance named Andrew for St Andrew's Day, then became Nicholas for December 6th. He decided to stay put till Christmas Eve. In the nursing home, I came round to the sound of church bells and a feather-light fall of snow. A dark-haired nurse came into the room with a sprig of mistletoe. "It's a boy!" she said joyfully, holding out the baby. "And a lucky one; he was born in a caul,[35] so he'll never be drowned." Momentarily, I was disappointed; I'd so much wanted a girl. But, strangely, an instant rapport sprang up between us. We called him Richard Noel.

However unmaternal I might have been, I was immensely

[35] Caul, a piece of membrane that can cover a newborn's head and face immediately after birth.

106

proud of our two boys, and as they grew older, loved taking them about to tea-parties, fairgrounds and horse shows. Martin's first ride ended in a fall which put him off, not only from the pony but from riding. He was a thoughtful boy, and even when at the village school, as they both were, instead of playing on the green after school, he'd run upstairs to the attic in order to read the newspaper. Richard, on the other hand, was away over the fields, looking for birds nests, catching frogs and tadpoles, and collecting acorns and nuts, all in due season.

Chapter 10

Outbreak of War,
Journalism, New Relationships

In spite of a mother's help, our babies anchored me at home while Aubrey was free to pursue his own activities. Adult courses were fewer in those days and in any case, Aubrey needed the car. So instead of taking up a hobby, I grew restless, unable without stimulus, even to practise the piano or write. This state of mind grew worse with the onset of war in 1939. Aubrey was in charge of six mills – a far more harassing job than joining the forces, which he wanted to do. But while his two brothers and a cousin served in the army, his father ordered Aubrey to man the mills, keeping the work force and machinery going, spinning threads of the finest Egyptian cotton, some of which was made into parachute cloth. Out of this came the finest cotton in the world and I had blouses made – blouses that never wore out.

Added to this demanding work, Aubrey was Major in charge of the Local Defence Volunteers as they were then known. Churchill later changed this clumsy name to the Home Guard. He was out, after long days at the mill, five nights in the week – one night all night, returning for breakfast with a tired yet always cheerful face. A man in a thousand! My war work was miniscule. Though two boys of 7 and 4 did require much attention, I joined the WVS[36] and three times a week worked in the Horwich British Restaurant. This entailed waiting on or washing up – with two helpers – for 270 people.

In these circumstances I saw less and less of Aubrey who, when he did return home was too tired for anything but sleep. If I wanted to speak to him, I had to ring him up at the mill. At home there was no conversation. Though fully occupied, I felt that life had become arid. As far as communication was concerned, it was like living in a desert. "But you have the children," friends reminded me, and "Remember there's a war on!" I needed no reminding and realised more and more, Aubrey's loyalty and willing service for everyone and everything. He never thought about himself. I was in default for grudging his life lived apart from me.

As I've explained, we lived in the hamlet of Rivington and had survived for five years without electricity or water. So the onset of war found us used to inconvenience and hard living. Clothing rations were no problem; there were jumble sales and 'exchanges'. Food, though restricted, was adequate: 2 oz each of butter and tea, 4 oz each of sugar and meat were allowed each week. Fruits and vegetables were scarce and expensive.

Life, of necessity, was bleak for everyone in the 1940s starting with the Great Snow when we in the village had to pull sledges 2½ miles into Horwich to collect meagre rations, including paraffin for lamps and heaters. In any case, we were allowed only 1½ gallons of petrol a week which enabled Aubrey to drive the 2 miles to the bus and on to the mill. I had the car twice a week; otherwise it was the bicycle with an outsize shopping basket.

Most of all, I missed what social life there had been – even

[36] Women's Voluntary Service, founded in 1936 by Stella Isaacs, Marchioness of Reading.

those boring dinner parties seemed desirable – because no one could get anywhere unless 'in' with the Black Market. And to be cut off by three hard winters added to the discomfort. One blessed interlude is worth recalling. This was a trip to London in 1941 to see *The Cherry Orchard* with John Gielgud and Peggy Ashcroft. With two friends I took a train and arrived in time for dinner and a sherry at a Lyons' restaurant. We then travelled by bus to the theatre which seemed to us like a glimpse of Paradise, worth the return journey at midnight, to arrive home, cold and weary at five in the morning. It was worth, even more, the cost of the adventure which amounted to twenty-seven shillings. This was the equivalent of one pound and thirty-five pence by the standards of 1992, fifty-one years later.

Beginning with this, the war years had many surprises. Early in 1942, again in London, I met Frank Singleton. He took me for dinner at the Cafe Royal. Barrel-shaped and rubicund, he was by far the most entertaining person I'd ever met, bubbling with literary anecdotes of people he knew from the theatre and literary worlds – James Agate, Dadie Rylands, Raymond Mortimer, Rosamond Lehmann, Cecil Day Lewis and the editors, it seemed, of every newspaper and journal. He himself had recently been assistant editor of *The Spectator* and overseas editor for the BBC. Son of a brushmaker in Bolton, this extraordinary man became president of the Cambridge Union, a fact of which we were constantly reminded. At this time, having achieved what he desired from life in London, he decided to return home to edit a local paper the *Bolton Evening News*.

I've no idea how he came to know of me or why he invited me to dinner. I'd written nothing except a few poems – in *The Spectator*, *The Observer*, *Times Literary Supplement*, and one or two others. And these according to my brother-in-law were accepted only 'because Phoebe is young and pretty.' Even more astounding was Frank's suggestion at the end of dinner, by which time he was bubbling over with more than enthusiasm: "I'd like you to be Women's Page editor of the *Bolton Evening News*."

So it came about. As soon as he was ensconced in the Bolton newspaper, Frank rang me up: "All I have to do now is to persuade the Chairman," he said. It turned out that the Chairman was a stately cousin of Lord Leverhulme whose only objection to the idea was, not my inexperience, but a personal matter. "Which toilet will she use?" he asked. The editorial board, all men, had a superior lavatory upstairs while the 'workers', including the women had the railway station variety on the ground floor. It was a pertinent question because had I not settled happily for the latter, embarrassment would have ensued and prevented his assent to my engagement.

After the initial delight at the prospect of a new and meaningful life, doubt set in. I'd not only no experience in journalism; with the exception of school essays, I'd written nothing. It was then that Frank's Pygmalion complex emerged. "I will teach you to write good prose, and to be a journalist," he promised. "You'll spend three months in the reader's room, longer in the sub-editors; you'll cover women's events such as bazaars and all social affairs. You'll write half a column on well-known townswomen each week and a special article of local interest – about 750 words. Meanwhile, you'll also learn shorthand and improve your typing." I was speechless and longed to withdraw. My return home that first evening was to know that home was where I belonged and domestic monotony to be envied above all else. My decision to refuse the job was strengthened by learning that I was about to step into the shoes of the renowned Mary Stott who was to become Women's Page Editor of the *Manchester Guardian* newspaper.

My halting withdrawal was met by brisk refusal: "Nonsense! It's a chance never to be repeated. I've never yet failed to make a journalist of someone I've marked down." I certainly felt marked down, pinned by an arrow to the ground. Wearing a white blouse made from Aubrey's parachute cloth, I was shown into the office the following week. This I shared with Frank's secretary Josephine, a pale fair girl, soon to break down under the yoke of Frank's demands. Before long, she gave in and left, the third girl to suffer a nervous breakdown in his service. Thereafter he employed a man.

Frank behind his desk was a wholly different man from Frank across the dinner table. Some days, the kindest and most understanding friend and teacher; others like a whiplash. On one of the latter, he rang for me. I'd written what I thought a good article and entered his office in high anticipation. Through glinting spectacles his cold seagulls' eyes hypnotised me. "Take this away!" He thrust the article at me, "I don't want fine writing; I want clear simple prose which has something to say, and says it in words well-chosen, apt and pared to a minimum." I left the room in silence, sat down and wrote it again to achieve the verdict: "Not bad but not good either!" Accustomed to his scalding tongue alternating with rare moments of praise, I learned, painfully, how to write. In this I was greatly helped by James, a young Adonis who was at least six years younger than me and worked in the library.[37] He corrected my errors of fact and read through every article with helpful suggestions. More than this, James showed interest, even pleasure, in my poems. It was he who brought comfort after Frank's outbursts and read through my proofs at lunchtime. We'd started lunching together, usually at a dark, oak-beamed pub in Bolton. Occasionally, in summer, we took lunch out, sitting in a park or a field.

At some stage he invited me home to meet his mother who, to my surprise, encouraged our friendship. It was some time before I learned that he was a schizophrenic. So far, I'd known

[37] Adonis, Greek mythology, god of beauty and desire.

only his attractive side, added to by his appearance. Tall, with curly hair, cornflower blue eyes, and a beautiful voice, he was a charmer and highly intelligent too. He'd read History at Cambridge, though his main interests were English and Psychology. Underneath all this, I felt there was something unhealthy in his morbid interest in women, something of the hot-house. This led me to prevaricate and turn his mind in other directions. Though his two older brothers were married and normal, he was of another genre. Again I turned to the image of the hot-house plant – something grown out of time and place, not quite healthy. There were days when I felt like a rabbit bewitched and compelled by an exotic snake.

As I might have expected, he wanted to go to bed with me. Although I wondered whether it could have amounted to anything more than that, I refused. I also refused to go to his home unless his mother was there. Quite often, he came to me in Rivington for a walk. This exercise showed me plainly that he was not a countryman. Returning to Aubrey was like breathing fresh air after the claustrophobic hot-house.

And yet there was something missing in my life. I had a huge yearning for something I knew not what. Even at the age of 20, I had to ask my sister-in-law a question which made her gaze at me with astonishment and pity. "Don't you know?" Of course I knew the mechanisms but nothing more, nothing about feelings. Even after marriage, instinct told me that I was missing something. With the war years and the increasing division in our lives, it seemed that we were hardly married at all. Just two people sharing the same house. Aubrey, with far greater responsibility and his pleasure in men's company, whether at the mill or in clubs of all kinds, was apparently content with the minimal relationship which I found so unfulfilling and disappointing. Gradually I became dependent on James's companionship while at the same time despising the man who wasn't quite a man. Not only had he a probing, questing mind, he understood women; he made me feel 'special'. Here was a person of great gifts wasted, thoughtful in unexpected ways. For instance he reproached me for not stamping a letter on the top right-hand corner. "Letters go through a machine; you're making it difficult for the operator." He seemed to read my thoughts and anticipate every move.

One spring day, after we'd known each other for about two years, he invited me to lunch at home. To my dismay, when I arrived, he greeted me with "Mother's out for the day!" I nearly turned away, but asked if Doris the maid was in. Unwisely, hearing she was, I went inside and was relieved that she served the lunch. No sooner had she left the room than James produced a bottle of Moet. Sip by sip, we finished it off and with the last sip James gleefully announced: "Doris has gone out!"

It was then I realised how alcohol weakens the will, for against my will, softened partly by pity, largely by champagne, and weary of saying 'no', I allowed him to carry me upstairs. For me, it was wholly unsatisfactory; as I'd suspected, he was impotent. And yet, not then, but later he woke me to what I'd been missing in 13 years of married life. Exultation was drowned in guilt. I felt actual pain at seeing Aubrey's face, pale from weariness on returning from work, or from a long evening on the Home Guard. Never once did he complain. "What a man!" I thought. "How he deserves love and encouragement." I certainly loved him, perhaps more than ever even as I betrayed him. I told James he must never come to our house again, that this relationship must end. But it didn't end because we met at work, and his charm worked insidiously on my conscience. His mother became uneasy when she realised I was keeping him at bay. "Please do go on seeing James," she said. "Your friendship matters so much. It keeps him on an even keel." Still I tried to stop his visits. After a few "nos" from me, he arrived one summer afternoon at the door. I was

114

driven to ask Aubrey to stop him from coming. "No, that's your job," he said, quite rightly. I despised myself as well as James for surrendering, for being totally engulfed, and dragged from action I should have taken, by a basic need.

Then I discovered I was pregnant. Even worse, I didn't know who by. But I did know I was in hell. What Aubrey thought I daren't ask or think, but I knew his suspicion, even more painful for being unuttered. I told him I was going to have an abortion and because he made no objection, I felt he had doubts himself. We could neither of us speak to the other about it, or ourselves or our feelings; this made me realise the gulf in our relationship. It was a cold, raw evening in February; I went by myself to a woman who lived at No 22 Daffodil Street. In my darkness and misery, I remember thinking how ironic was this name, with the spring flowers only a month away. Afterwards I fainted and was violently sick, then ruthlessly bundled into my car, and given a card on which were written two words: 'Parcel delivered.'

I find it impossible to write more of this horror story in which some stranger played the leading part. The one shaft of light, then, was my long and rewarding friendship with Frank and my dearest friend, Rachel, whom he had married, following a meeting and dinner at our house. This was a happy outcome of those few terrible years. They stood by me, reproved and comforted me, Rachel insisting that it was wrong to continue a relationship merely in order to keep the man sane. One day, Frank sent for me in the office. He'd had a visit from a great friend of mine, Dr Joseph Silverston (nicknamed JD), Superintendent of Lancaster Moor Mental hospital to whom, in my desperation, I'd confided my sad story. Somehow he had contrived to meet James and at once got the measure of him. "You must make Phoebe break off relations with him." JD told Frank. "He's no good, totally shored up, and will drag her down and ruin her marriage." Such was his agitation, he cut himself while shaving.

115

In the wretched blur of the following months, I cannot remember the sequence of events. It felt as though I no longer belonged to myself, but had been taken over, if not by evil itself, by something whose tentacles grasped me in a sort of primal darkness and slime.

Turning thankfully from this once again to the bright side: my special articles in the paper were becoming popular, even more so than Frank's, I was told, which were too literary for the general public. And I started writing scripts for the radio – and on writers, for Woman's Hour.[38] Also at this time, Frank introduced me to several, mostly literary, celebrities, who spent weekends with him and Rachel. Through him, I met Rupert Hart-Davis,[39] who became a lifelong friend, and my publisher.

Before long, Frank initiated the Pleiades Club – whose members were intellectual men – and who met for drinks at their house followed by dinner out. I was occasionally invited and enlivened by his 'star' London friends. Rachel bore the brunt of all this. As many as thirty high-powered men would arrive at 6.00 p.m. for exotic drinks and tit-bits. An hour and a half later, they would leave a disordered room and empty or half-empty glasses. On one occasion, after the men had departed, leaving a trail of debris for her to clear up, she took one look round and, inwardly raging, picked up every part-filled glass and drank the contents, hurling the last one at the window. Thereupon, she passed out. Consternation ensued when Frank returned with their weekend guest, a high court judge. Together they picked her up and put her to bed, consoling themselves with whisky among the litter.

Drink and extravagance were to contribute to Frank's downfall. When, sometime in the 1950s, Rachel inherited a quarter of a million pounds, she immediately made ten

[38] Woman's Hour, BBC radio programme.
[39] Sir Rupert Hart-Davis, British publisher, editor, man of letters, 1907-1999.

thousand of it over to Frank. This was gone within a year. One of the first things he did was to rent a suite at the Savoy where he lavishly entertained his friends. To think that only ten years previously, Rachel and I had jaunted to London for a weekend during the war and were hard pressed to find twenty-five shillings for bed and breakfast at the Mayfair.

By this time, I was rid of my daemon; James told me he was going to marry a girl in the office. He was drinking heavily, and when a friend rang to enquire after him, Doris answered and replied: "Mr James is surrounded by bottles." A few months later, when I heard he'd put his head in the gas oven, I wasn't unduly upset.

Chapter 11

Herbert Palmer,
Literary Encounters

Moving on, I immersed myself in my job at the newspaper and the care of my husband and two young boys. I had little enough time for writing. My special articles were mostly formulated in my head as I sat in the tram, after parking my bicycle on the way to the office. Frank had initiated me in the art of mentally producing articles of the right length till they virtually wrote themselves. "Store in your mind all you want to say and sleep on it." I knew some journalists used to write notes in the evening, set them aside, and by some magic, in the morning, the article was written. And by this magic, sometimes poems are written. One of mine evolved something like this: the opening lines 'Between waking and sleep I am alone in a bright field' drifted into my mind on the brink of sleep. When I awoke, the poem *The Horses* clamoured to be written.[40] It became one of my most successful – for radio and various poetry collections.

I left the newspaper in 1945 and henceforth, through poetry, was led to one of the most momentous periods of my life. In

[40] 'The Horses' in *Preparing To Leave*, published by Enitharmon, 1977.

1946, after my first reading to the Poetry Society, the poet Herbert Palmer introduced himself to me. "You must be a reincarnation of Emily Brontë!" were almost his first words. Thereafter, he followed me, tutored me in the art of poetry and prose and pushed me into the notice of editors to an almost embarrassing degree. He became my mentor and devoted friend. Herbert, whose nickname was Tarka (he looked so like an otter) was a great angler. For a time he was fishing correspondent to the *Manchester Guardian* and author of a splendid book *The Roving Angler*.

When he discovered I lived in Rivington, an angler's semi-paradise with its four reservoirs, he invited himself to stay. And stay he did, three times a year. He earned his keep, not so much in bringing trout home, as in his help, guidance, and insistence that my poems must appear in every possible magazine, and eventually in a collection. Almost entirely due to him, my first hardback, *Lean Forward Spring* was published in 1948. Tarka, a friend of the Irish mystic poet AE,[41] who claimed to see fairies, was an ardent believer in the spirit world either of fairies or angels, certain that we live on spiritually after death of the body.

Tarka, who could be as gentle as a dove, had his wolf-like side. With his wild grey hair, yellow teeth, and fiery brown eyes, there was something apocalyptic about him. He was like an Old Testament prophet, deeply religious, living with one foot in the spirit world. He had an unfailing knack of rubbing editors up the wrong way, scorning them as opportunists, sycophants, who sucked up to the famous and/or popular writers of the day.

I introduced Tarka to Frank Singleton who found him highly diverting, and asked the three of us to dinner. His wife Rachel had prepared a sumptuous meal. Not only did we

[41] AE: Pseudonym of George William Russell, Anglo-Irish writer, editor and poet, 1867–1935.

enjoy excellent food but wine in plenty. Tarka quaffed several glasses of sherry before enjoying a subtle beef and mushroom dish with a fine St Emilion. "I drink wine like beer!" he laughed as his glass was refilled. We got onto the subject of contemporary poetry; "No spirit light in it." he declared. "It's too self-conscious and written with the top half of their brains." "Well, how about Eliot?"[42] Frank inquired. "Eliot!" Tarka shot up from the table like a firework, "I took him to pieces, annihilated, and completely demolished him in my lecture at St Alban's!" Thereupon he sat down with a bump, ruefully concluding: "And they only gave me three guineas for it!"

Tarka was determined to introduce me to the literary world and our friendship led to an introduction to the Celtic Twilight (Irish Literary Renaissance) Group of poets.[43] Tarka suggested a meeting with Seamus O'Sullivan,[44] one of the last stars of this group. With this in mind, Aubrey and I took the boys on holiday to Ireland in the summer of 1946. We stayed a few miles north of Dublin in the lovely Portmarnock Hotel on the coast. During our stay, Seamus rang inviting me to his stately Georgian home. On the proposed day, Seamus rang again to say he was unwell but a younger well-known poet who I'll call Patrick MacDonald would meet me instead. So it was. I arrived at Jury's Hotel one August evening. A smallish, dark-haired man with a typically Irish face got up to greet me, led me to a table and ordered drinks. "I was rather apprehensive of this meeting," he began. "Seamus told me you had a voice like a sergeant-major!" Feeling rather damped at this, I sat down and for an hour we talked formally of poets and poetry. He made no particular impression on me, so I was very surprised when he rang up the next day suggesting we meet for drinks at

[42] T.S. Eliot, British poet, dramatist, literary critic, 1888–1965.
[43] Celtic Twilight, nickname for Irish Literary Renaissance.
[44] Seamus O'Sullivan, real name James Sullivan Starkey. Irish poet, 1879–1958.

the Portmarnock Club. Again the talk was impersonal and desultory. A few days later, we had a moonlit walk along the shore, and sat for a while on the sand hills gazing out to sea.

At the end of our week's family holiday, we sailed for home and I felt I would never see Patrick again. So I was surprised and delighted to receive a letter from him. I had never received such a letter – one that only a poet could write. A really good letter makes you feel you are in the room with the writer. That he is talking to you and no one else and that you matter and share his thoughts. It's a letter that evokes a response to be reread and kept. Of course I replied, tuning in to his thoughts. Slowly I realised that one can fall in love through letters. Indeed, such harmony and response was generated that I felt a solid presence would intrude and break a magic spell. Yet week by week, as we drew closer through the written word, we both began to long for the actual voice and touch. I found myself racing home if I felt a letter was due; enduring days of frustration if nothing came.

September turned into a nostalgic and haunting October which glowed with a golden St Luke's summer. Somehow it was suggested that I could meet Seamus and his friends before winter set in. How could I explain another visit to Ireland to Aubrey? But somehow I did. And this time I did meet Seamus O'Sullivan and other fine poets. The talk, accompanied by soft lighting, a crackling log and peat fire, and whisky, was spiced with Irish wit. I felt that Celtic Twilight was an apt description of this last age of a period of great Irish poetry and song with the Master W.B. Yeats, living only in the memory of those present.

I spent that night at a dreary commercial hotel, an effective dampener of every kind of spirit. But Patrick had told me to meet him the next morning at the St Stephen's Green bus stop. It was a diamond day with drops of recent rain sparkling from every leaf. Patrick directed me on to a bus, and I felt as though I was someone else, playing a part I had not rehearsed.

f

The drive to Glendalough in County Wicklow was all part of this dream with the old bus rattling its way through wooded country, wild fields and glens. Leaves swirled aslant as we passed, and there were long unprogrammed stops at pubs, followed by reluctant grinding gears. We passed through tunnels of trees, red-gold-brown in the sun, and along roads lined with their colours. On a stretch almost waist-deep in leaves, was a man sweeping, his barrow under a great arch of branches, piled up and toppling. "Trying to sweep up the leaves of Wicklow with one small broom," Patrick smiled as he lit a pipe.

The descent into Glendalough was magic. Without the tourist attractions of today's world, it was a vale of myth and legend. We stayed at the Royal Hotel, quiet, unpretentious, whose few guests were mostly elderly ladies, curious to know who we were and where we came from. Patrick had told them that we came from Belfast. That evening, I let slip that I hunted with a pack of harriers. "Oh," exclaimed a sharp-faced spinster. "Do tell us which pack you hunt with. I don't know of any in Belfast." That was a real stopper. This was after dinner in the lounge where the smoke from a wood fire bothered me. "Come outside," Patrick rescued me. "The smoke is getting in your eyes." Thereafter, we were viewed with deep suspicion.

The memory of those few days remains even 46 years on as I write now. The gloomy lake, sometimes silvered with shafts of light; the sandy road alongside looking up to Lugnaquilla – Ireland's highest mountain – ever changing colour, the Lakeside Hotel where we stopped for tea with hot scones in front of a peat fire. Everywhere we walked, the blue smoke spiralled above the trees, a pageant of colours from yellows through coppers and reds, dark as blood. One day we sat on a pile of logs and I said, "Thirty or more years on, I'll look back and live again in this moment." And I have, but could only enshrine it in poetry:

122

Blue puddles of inverted sky
Blue smoke blue
A curlew's cry
Come back and haunt me still

Following this magical stay with Patrick, I knew that we must meet again and made plans to visit before the end of the year. Tarka, who felt himself responsible for my meeting with Patrick, had advised that I tell Aubrey about my proposed visit. I knew he was right and wondered why it was so difficult; impossible to talk to Aubrey on any intimate subject. There was a barrier between us; and though I'd always known we were not on the same wavelength, by now I was half-afraid, half-ashamed, and fearful of causing someone so clear and simple, painful embarrassment. Moreover I loved him. If I'd been more honest, I would by now, have admitted my relationship with Patrick was far more powerful than a merely physical one. Patrick himself described it: "There's something mystic in what I feel for you." So I was possessed by an emotion quite outside my will-power to escape.

In December 1946, after visiting poets and editors in London, I took the boat train to North Wales and the night crossing to Ireland. It was a rough night with a force nine gale blowing. I spent it on the top deck, which was deserted, lying down on a hard bench, not being ill.

I met Patrick and again we stayed at Glendalough, walking the stormy glen, leafless now, and still lovely with flurries of snow, and the blue smoke swirling among the bare branches. I remember climbing up a bank and looking down on the lake, black and restless like shined silk. A robin perched on a larch beside us and sang his two-pebble winter song. It seemed like a foreboding. On my return, Aubrey was full of concern, asking questions which I couldn't answer. I was a divided person, longing for one, and belonging to the other.

Chapter 12

Richard's Illness and Death

During the winter of 1947, our son Richard – who had become prone to persistent ear infections – developed a series of abscesses, causing distress for us all. It was before the general use of penicillin, but the doctor prescribed M and B.[45] Never well, Richard rarely complained and finally, he had an operation for mastoiditis in the right ear. The trouble continued through 1947 and early 1948. It was a nightmare. In 1948 he had another mastoid operation, this time on the left ear. Some weeks later he had radical mastoid surgery. This time it was critical. Aubrey and I sat watching the clock in the hospital waiting room. I noticed a white lilac ruffled in the wind between returning to the black clock fingers.

Eventually the door opened and the surgeon, though non-committal, said we might see him. White-faced, head swathed in bandages, he was still unconscious. It was a long hard grind to recovery. I visited him every day, and felt torn apart by his brave smile. "The dressings are very painful," the nurse said. "But he's a wonderful patient – never cries out like the Hurricane pilot next door." It seemed as though convalescence

---

[45] M and B: Sulfonamide, sulfa drug, one of a large group of drugs used to treat bacterial infection.

would never end. Anxiety beset us throughout the year; I could think of little else. It was very hard on Martin who must have felt left out, neglected, during this period. During the crisis time, he stayed with his Aunt Mary, Aubrey's sister; and here he too developed a severe ear and throat infection. Mary believed it was in protest at the devoted attention paid to his brother. Later I came to think that his reserve, sometimes antagonism, stemmed from this unhappy time.

In the late spring of 1948, when Richard seemed recovered, the doctor suggested we send him further south to boarding school. "This damp climate obviously doesn't suit him." With the greatest reluctance, we took him away from his tutor where he was doing well, and sent him to a progressive school – St Christopher's, Letchworth in Hertfordshire.

Emerging from this rough period, we were both in need of a holiday. On impulse, I suggested we go to Iona, a small island off the West Coast of Scotland. It seemed the right place to give thanks for Richard's recovery and to recover ourselves. I wrote asking for rooms. There was only one farm on the whole island which had a single free week that summer. So it was. I booked at Sithean, which means Hill of the Angels. To my dismay, I found that week included Richard's half term weekend. He wrote begging us to come to school and take him out for the autumn half-term instead.

Iona in June is at its best – long days more often than not sunny, with glorious sunsets. It's an island of miniature magnificence – nothing high or daunting, yet the rocky limestone cliffs seem almost formidable in wildness and grandeur. We loved the clean-washed white sand, the sheep-cropped turf and wild flowers. Green clefts, riven by quick, clear streams, running to the sea were massed with yellow flag irises. Though we knew no one, we were soon made welcome by members of the Iona Community who invited us to coffee or tea parties. There was no alcohol on the island which was blessed, also, with only three cars. We couldn't have chosen a better place for peace and refreshment.

On the first Sunday, June 13th, we went to the service at the Abbey. Never having taken communion in a Presbyterian church, I was baffled when a great hunk of bread was passed to me from the end of the pew. Used to the wafer taken at the Altar, and realising I must put bread in my mouth, I took an enormous bite when my neighbour nudged me to pass it on. We came out, exhilarated by Dr George McLeod's talk and the bright sun. "What an apt text!" I exclaimed to Aubrey, "I reckon the sufferings of this present time are not worthy of the joy to come." It was the epistle from Romans 8 for Sunday June 13th. St Paul certainly had a word for us. A few minutes later, I picked up something shining on the sandy path. "What luck!" I said, holding up a three penny bit. It seemed at last that everything had come right with Richard recovered and happy at school.

We spent a long lazy afternoon, rambling around Sithean and down to the sea. That evening there was a glowing sunset; we decided to walk into it, facing Ireland and the Mountains of Mourne. It seemed like a blessing. As we turned reluctantly homeward, a shepherd, who was our host came to meet us. I thought this unusual. As he drew near in the gathering shadows, he spoke to Aubrey. "Can I have a word with you?" I wondered what he could possibly have to say but caught a few words: "Your boy – bathing." I knew in a flash – Richard had been drowned.

It is impossible to describe the stunning shock and grief of the days, months and more that followed. At first the terrible news and its implications was impossible to absorb as was the long journey home. My father and Elaine were waiting at Preston railway station. I cannot write of that meeting; the recapitulation is too painful to experience, even as I write now in 1990, 42 years later.

Three days passed before the clay pit where Richard lay yielded up his body. Because of his ear operations, he was the only one unable to swim among the three boys paddling in the shallow end. It was a dangerous pit forbidden by the school, but being half term, the master in charge had taken the boys there for a picnic. Seeing an unauthorised group of girls at the far end, the master left the boys, telling them not to go in the water. It was a hot day; they were alone, and all three jumped in. The other two scrambled out and heard Richard shouting, "Help! Help, I'm drowning!" They thought he was fooling. "The last we saw of him," said one boy, "was his hand waving and a wisp of hair above the water." Two Air Force pilots, both strong swimmers, were sitting a few yards away from the scene.

Aubrey was required to go to the mortuary to identify his body. I'm ashamed to say that I was too much of a coward to accompany him. More than ever, I realised how much I owed to Aubrey, and how ashamed I felt at having betrayed him.

Fortunately the relationship with Patrick was over. Quite rightly, he'd decided he couldn't leave his wife – she had refused to give him a divorce. And of course, had it come to the crunch, I couldn't possibly have left Aubrey and the boys. Now in indescribable misery, I saw Richard's death as retribution. Through his illness, we had grown so close as to be part of one another and, as his teachers remarked, he was an unusual and gifted boy. During the holiday prior to his last term, we had played a 'questions and answers' game with a group of 12-15 year old children. Richard's questions were quite different and somewhat disquieting. "Who is going to die first in our family?" and so on. Once, when saying goodnight to me, he asked, "Mummy, when I'm dead, will I be able to walk through walls?"

Shortly after term began, he wrote that his bicycle brakes were faulty. This fact was recalled when, after much persuasion, I went to see a medium at the College for Spiritual and Psychical Studies in London. I expected nothing and felt that this was the wrong thing to do. After feeling her way, the medium realised that I had come hoping for reassurance regarding my son. She felt at the back of both her ears before saying he'd had complications following ear trouble. And then "I see water surrounding him; he was drowned." Then a pause and then: "He thought it would happen on his bicycle going downhill." Until then, I had forgotten this fact and therefore it impressed me more than anything.

After such a tragedy, everyone goes through the preceding events wondering why it happened. Reproaches and self-blame are common. "We shouldn't have taken that holiday; we should have taken him out." A reproach hammered in like a nail when I read his last letter lying open on the piano when we returned from Iona. "Please come and take me out. You haven't been to a half term at school yet. I've worked out the trains from Manchester." Those words haunt me yet. I counted the chance events that led to the fatal happening. Had it not been such a hot day the boys wouldn't have gone swimming; had the master obeyed school rules, they wouldn't have gone to the pit. Then of course, "why did we choose that school?" There were thirteen happenings that led to the tragedy. "Is there purpose and providence in life?" I asked. "Or are we victims of blind chance?" It seemed at the time that everything pointed in the one direction.

Although I was thankful that Patrick had broken the link between us, I'd felt hollow at the loss even before the far heavier loss of Richard. An avenging angel hovered around as I remembered my last meeting with Patrick in London. We saw Margot Fonteyn and Robert Helpmann in the ballet *Giselle*. As the dramatic first act ended in tragedy, I felt we too were doomed.

Another disappointment was to come in 1949. I had a

miscarriage. Nature, who knows best, decided I was in no fit state to bear a child. And this one, ironically, I had so much hoped for. It seemed there was a pattern being woven of which, at the time, I was unconscious. Many people, in the arms of grief, fly to God for comfort. All I could see was that life is worked out for us beyond the exercise of free will which by no means grants us our desires. No, I thought, we cannot do it all ourselves.

Meanwhile, Martin, aged 15, had been at Haileybury Public School since the end of the war in 1945. There were about forty red-blanketed beds in his dormitory which reminded me of a prison camp. If a progressive school was an unfortunate choice for Richard, this spartan school was equally wrong for Martin, who became more than ever withdrawn and inhibited. He, poor boy, was quite unable to give any indication of his feelings about Richard's going. Feelings buried deep which manifested in his going bald soon after the tragedy. Again he must have felt left out by our grief and recriminations, our total preoccupation with his younger brother. I was at the time, blinded to this fact, to my lasting regret.

Chapter 13

Catherine's Birth and Early Years

When, in the spring of 1949 I became pregnant, it was natural that Martin, in his final years at Haileybury Boarding School, should feel resentment. Before my knowledge of the pregnancy, I had a rewarding holiday in Austria with Aubrey, his brother John and my friend Hazel. It began for me with the little black train of open carriages, spitting sparks like fireflies as it chugged its way up to St Wolfgang. It felt like turning over the pages from a tale of woe and horror to an enchanted land. The lake itself, a dark jewel set amid trees and mountains, shone in beams of light from the White Horse Inn. Our room looked out over the lake and I had the distinction of sleeping in the bed recently occupied by the actor Dennis Price while he was making a film.[46] "You have new bedding," the receptionist informed me. "The man burned his bed," then she whispered, "The drink and the cigarettes."

An unforgettable memory was of getting lost in a vast forest. Hazel and I had lagged behind the men, and suddenly realised we were separated by the dark dusky silence among

[46] Dennis Price, British actor, 1915-1973.

huge pine trees. After some time trekking down alternative paths, we became really frightened – like Hansel and Gretel without any comforting breadcrumbs to lead us home. Time became irrelevant; all we knew was the sun's withdrawal from the clearings which taunted us with hopes of freedom. It seemed a very long time before thudding footsteps on the pine-needles made us halt in expectation. Aubrey, his face beetroot coloured and streaming with sweat, eyes shining with relief, appeared as an angel of deliverance. Again, as many times before, I was shot through with remorse to realise what I meant to him, and equally, what he meant to me.

We drank beer at the Zumbaren Inn with its clean scrubbed wooden tables. The shiny glittering pans in peasants' houses were a sight to behold. We marvelled at the fireflies by night and the mountain snows and alpenrosen flowers by day. Climbing Patscherkofel, the highest mountain from Igls, I began to feel sick. Hazel scorned my suggestion of pregnancy. "You can't possibly feel sick yet!" she said. I'd only just missed my first period, but so it was. I was delighted to feel ill and unable to enjoy coffee and croissants at an outside café in Paris on the return journey.

Nine months later, February 2nd 1950 came with snow. Despite being heavily pregnant, I set out in wellington boots for my beloved moors, returning to the road by jumping off a stone wall. That evening we had friends in for drinks. Suddenly, to my consternation, the waters broke with a wallop onto the carpet. The doctor groaned when I rang him up. "A dry birth. Not good," he exclaimed. And I had had my forty-first birthday a few days before. Some hours later, the well-known labour pains began. Aubrey drove me into hospital and stayed with me until about 1.30 a.m. By now, I was well on with contractions. "The baby will be here in half an hour," the doctor assured me. But I laboured in vain and the doctor grew anxious. At about 4 a.m. he told me he'd have to do a caesarean. How I hated trundling down to the operating theatre with its white walls, white figures, bright lights. I cried through a haze of drugs: "Put me under! Put me under!" So under I went and later awoke being violently ill while a nurse asked, "Will you 'ave fried fish for your breakfast?"

The beautiful auburn-haired baby had shot out onto the operating table only seconds before the descent of the poised knife. The day sister had visited me at the onset of labour. "Don't imagine you'll be able to breastfeed the baby at your age!" A few days later she came to ask me a favour. "We have premature twins, and the mother can't feed them. Would you be so kind?" I looked at her in amazement. "You see, you're the best cow in the hospital," she said. For my three children, I never had a bottle in the house; and they were breast-fed for nine months, taking mouthfuls of spinach between gulps.

When Catherine, as we called her, was about three weeks old, I crept into the drawing room where she lay – spread out on a shawl on the sofa. I found Martin running a forefinger up and down her front, a smile of wonderment on his face. "Don't tell me she was born in original sin," he said as he turned toward me. "I can't believe it!" he continued. This was a big problem settled. Later that year, Martin completed his higher education and returned home. Having decided on a career path, he left for Oxford to study at the College of Architecture. This move turned out to be a major turning point in his life.

Turning again to Catherine, the difficulty was my obsessive anxiety. Every spot, pimple, or snuffle filled me with dismay. "We can't go on like this," the district nurse exclaimed as I agonised over having her vaccinated. The shock of Richard's death still haunted me and its legacy shadowed Catherine's early years. Fortunately she was a happy, outgoing child who took great pleasure in neighbours' and visitors' company. As early as three years old, she'd escape from the carefully barricaded garden to call at the cottage next door, thus adding to my anxiety. Not without reason, because when she was eighteen months, a child from the village school had brought her home in her arms. She had been crawling in the middle of the road at Vicarage Corner, a dangerous bend around which motorists whirled as if they owned the place.

She loved the village school but paid scant attention to lessons. She loved, even more, release on to the Green to play with the other children – so different from Martin who, from an early age would run up the stairs, newspaper in hand, to the solitude of the attic. The next move, at eight years old, to the Bolton School Junior division, found her quite unable to reach the high standard required. As expected, she failed the eleven-plus and the entrance exam to the Senior division. Her gifts lay in other directions – a remarkable understanding of people and an ability to tune in with everyone. We had no choice, in view of the undesirable local secondary schools, but to send her to boarding school. This decision nearly killed me emotionally.

In our concern to find a school where she would be happy, we looked over no fewer than fifteen schools which were either academically 'out of reach', had poor discipline standards, or placed a heavy emphasis upon religion. Others we turned down for strange reasons: the obligation to supply ten pairs of red stockings or two pink eiderdowns, and suchlike conditions. Unwisely, we decided on a private school in Shropshire, chiefly because they kept riding ponies. Set in beautiful countryside, the school was run, seemingly, by two understanding spinsters who loved each other too well. At the end of a year, this school was the only one to close down.

In September 1963 we sent Catherine to a public boarding school in Northamptonshire. After three years she scraped through six GCSE exams and returned home to complete her higher education at a local college.[47]

[47] GCSE: General Certificate of Secondary Education

Chapter 14

Martin and Jutta

Turning to my son Martin, after a rigorous and difficult passage through adolescence, he proved that success can be achieved by hard work and determination. After finding an avenue for his creative and artistic talents, he left home in 1950 and studied at the Oxford College of Architecture. Having completed his academic course work, he returned home to take a year of Professional Practice with a company in Preston. In 1956 he joined the Royal Institute of British Architects.

Not only did he achieve academic success but during his years in Oxford, he met his future wife Jutta. They shared a love of art, music, and an overall passion for self-creativity. Jutta came to Oxford from Argentina to study Ceramics. While continuing her education at an English school in Buenos Aires, she spent time with a well-known sculptor. Truly inspired by this experience, Jutta pursued her creative talents in Oxford. Having met and fallen for Martin, she returned to Argentina in 1955 and set up a pottery studio where she designed and sold her products. Her best customer was a chocolatier who wanted to sell his chocolates in bowls made on a potter's wheel. Laughingly she said, "No wonder I'm a chocoholic!"

With his mind made up to follow Jutta, Martin learned to

speak and communicate in Spanish and continue his career in Architecture. We were terribly worried and felt that he was taking an enormous risk. But he left for Buenos Aires in 1956 and took a job with a company of architects. Meanwhile Jutta continued to design and sell pottery. She also exhibited her work with a group named 'Estudios de Bellas Artes'. Martin later told us that they planned to marry. For us to go to the wedding, we would have to travel by boat to South America. The cost and journey time were prohibitive so we decided to stay at home and drink to their health and happiness on our side of the Atlantic Ocean.

Looking back, I realise to my lasting regret, that I had not recognised Martin's emotional needs. Now that he had found his true love, I should have felt happy for him. Instead I was sad and resentful that he had chosen to leave home, live in a foreign country and marry a woman we had not met.

Martin and Jutta were married in Buenos Aires on May 3rd 1957. It was a beautiful wedding illustrated by the photographs we received. We also heard that among all the wedding speeches, Martin's was delivered in the most perfect Spanish. What a surge of pride this gave me!

They returned to Britain in July 1957 and stayed with us at Fisher House while Martin set up a business practice in Bolton. I recall my first meeting with Jutta and the apprehension we must have both felt. Attractive and well spoken, I was aware of her many talents and of course I recognised that she and Martin were well matched.

Jutta surely felt devastated to leave her home and adapt to a new way of life in a wet cold country. After three weeks, they moved into a small flat in Bolton where the grime of the north became apparent. After washing her curtains, Jutta was appalled to find them grimed with soot in no time at all. It was extremely difficult for them and, again looking back, I feel ashamed that we didn't offer additional support.

Much to his delight Martin found a job in Shrewsbury, so they moved south to a cleaner, more pleasant environment. On March 13th, 1961, their first son Francis was born in their new home. The day before his birth we had visited and this news took us by surprise! Jutta later remarked: "Francis was in a hurry!" We were so delighted that our first grandchild had arrived safely.

Their second son soon followed his brother into the world. He arrived on June 9th, 1963, and later Jutta commented, "Julian was in even more of a hurry!" Motherhood came naturally and she took it in her stride. We were thrilled and proud of our two grandsons. After a move to a newly built house in Birkenhead, the boys were educated at the local boys' school at which they achieved excellent results in their GCSE exams.

Francis and Julian have rewarding careers and grown into delightful young men. They have their own families and I am the proud great grandmother of five wonderful children.

While taking care of the family, Jutta found time to build her own career. In 1969 she took a three year teacher training course and wrote a thesis on 18th century English Literature. During her career she developed new and innovative teaching methods which have been put to use in many schools.

In 1964 the family moved to a large old house named Aston Lodge in Birkenhead. The house was first built in the 18th century after which came extensions to the original structure. They discovered a well underneath the kitchen floor which had been the original source of water. Martin put his architectural skills to work and while completely renovating the house, he made sure that the home retained its original character.

Martin set up his own business from Aston Lodge. While his main focus was housing, he designed sports facilities and a small factory. For many years Martin had endured the mental and emotional repercussions of his brother's death and I truly admire his courage and determination to succeed in life.

I remember family reunions and the dining room table overflowing with mouthwatering dishes carefully prepared by Jutta. Martin, a real wine connoisseur, provided red and white wines from all over the world. I have such happy memories of long sunny days at their home and also of their visits to our beloved Fisher House.

Chapter 15

Literary Highlights,
Rupert Hart-Davis

Returning to 1956, when Catherine was happily playing away sunlit days at the village school and Marjorie, a delightful girl, was caring for her at home. During the summer of 1956, I went to London where the PEN Conference was being held.[48] For me it was a week in the whirling excitement of another planet. It seemed every poet, editor and novelist was in London and to be met at parties, readings, lectures and dinners. Also in the Guildhall, Fishmonger's and Goldsmith's Halls, the University, and the Library.

The previous year I had met the handsome and gifted publisher and writer Rupert Hart-Davis who was to publish two collections of my poems: *The Buttercup Children*, and *Prayer For Sun*. Here I should say that four collections of poems had already been published. These included *Lean Forward Spring*, *Out Of The Dark*, and two other collections.

Rupert was out of town for a few days and invited me to make use of his flat in Soho Square. Before he left, we had a

[48] PEN: poets, playwrights, editors, essayists, novelists, (now known as PEN International.)

drink and a long talk during which, with his eager interest at the doings of others, he extracted the truth of my relationship with Patrick. One of his great charms was a sincere interest in others along with reticence about himself and his considerable achievements. He was one of those rare people who not only make you feel better than you are, but talk to you as if you were as knowledgeable as he.

Later in the week, Rupert gave a really memorable dinner party at the Garrick Club. This was to celebrate R.S. Thomas winning the Arts Council Prize for the year's best collection of poems.[49] The collection, *Song At The Year's Turning,* had just been published by Rupert.[50] He placed R.S. Thomas on my right at the dinner table. "For goodness sake," he said, "Do your best to get him to talk; he eschews wine and women – if not song!" Thomas was indeed a dour and mostly silent companion, no doubt assessing my inferior intellect. One of his observations does stick in my mind: "I always think it was strange of St Paul to say, "If a man loveth not his neighbour whom he hath seen, how shall he love God who he hath not seen?" I should have thought that, having seen his neighbour, a man might hope that God was a great deal better! He sipped sparingly of his wine, and addressed few remarks to anyone present. During the light-hearted talk, Rupert declared his own ability to assess a person's age. Unwisely I challenged him and evoked an immediate reply: "I should say you are forty-eight." As he was the only man ever to add an extra year to my actual age, I felt somewhat chagrined.

The year following, at the PEN conference, I was not surprisingly forty-eight and ready for the unexpected! I had the pleasure of indulging in tea and crumpets with the well-known and loved poet John Betjeman.[51] I'd never met anyone so

---

[49] Ronald Stuart Thomas, Welsh poet, Anglican priest, 1913-2000.

[50] *Song At The Year's Turning,* published by Hart-Davis, 1955.

[51] Sir John Betjeman, British poet/writer 1906–1984. Poet Laureate 1972-1984.

entertaining, so spontaneously witty and refreshing. All I remember now is that I seemed to fall in with his ideas and see life through his eyes. He insisted on showing me round his beloved St Bartholomew's church which was a stone's throw from his flat, and giving me its history in minute detail. I couldn't follow his example of crossing himself at intervals and bobbing before the altar but he led on enthusiastically, unaware of my 'low church' bewilderment. We returned to his flat for more talk. As I was leaving, he asked me to come to tea the following day. Another person who could make one feel good – more than good, happy.

A very different encounter was with Rosamond Lehmann who also asked me for tea in her flat in the region of Sloane Square.[52] She was a tall elegant figure floating around a spacious sitting room in rose-coloured chiffon. There was something abstracted and dreamy about her and her talk with me was largely concerned with her true preoccupations – her next novel and Cecil Day-Lewis[53] her acknowledged paramour. But she was charming to me, a raw newcomer to the literary scene; and talked of many who belonged there as though I too would know them. We got around to the subject of Rupert whom she liked and admired. "But", she added, "he is not a passionate man." When I felt that she might expand on this, she arose from her cushions and drifted backstage to make a pot of tea. Presently she handed me a delicate china cup of pale smoky liquid with a few twigs floating in it. It was the worst cup of tea I've ever tasted.

I remember one time while staying with Rupert, he said, "You're the sort of woman I might have married, but I'm a one-woman man." I admired him for that. This was after virtual separation from his second wife Comfort. They were later divorced.

[52] Rosamond Lehmann CBE, British novelist, 1901–1990.
[53] Cecil Day-Lewis, British poet, 1904–1972. Poet Laureate 1968–1972.

Rupert became deeply involved with his secretary Ruth Simon, whom he eventually married. I had stayed with Ruth on one of my London visits, and found her a delightful, restful companion. I visited them both in their tiny stone cottage high up on the fell-side in Swaledale.[54] What a contrast from London! Here there was only a cart-track to the road below which led to Hawes and no mod cons. There was certainly no water supply or lavatory, merely an earth closet at the field's edge. Ruth filled jam-jars with wild flowers, dropping petals and pollen everywhere. An old dresser displayed cottage china; a farm kitchen striking clock and primitive oil cooker supplied all their needs.

Even during the winter snows they fled to their enchanted hillside. Ruth described her pleasure in the lighted cottage windows across the valley. Each one, as the time drew near, displaying a Christmas tree shining with tinsel and coloured baubles.

I never saw a happier couple. They could sit together all evening in perfect harmony without speaking a word. Shortly after one of my visits, Rupert received his knighthood. This was followed by their attending a wedding in Edinburgh. Ruth, in all her finery, was in high spirits, laughing as she stepped into the taxi to the church. "I couldn't believe it," Rupert told me afterwards. "She suddenly said 'Oh!' as she turned toward me and died in my arms."

They'd been married just two and a half years. It was a most stunning blow. He arranged for her to be buried on the banks of the River Swale in the field outside their garden. A plain stone bore a couplet from *In Memoriam*. Rupert said, "I wept and wept in desperation."

Letters both of congratulation and sympathy poured in. Rupert was quite unable to cope with these and the disposing of Ruth's possessions. The only solution was to find another

[54] Swaledale, North Yorkshire National Park, UK.

secretary from his firm to help him out. So arrived June, kind, capable, and seventeen years younger. She took over, not only as secretary but as manager of his household. As well as undertaking all the shopping and cooking, she would ward off unwelcome calls and visitors. She was a jewel, an answer to a prayer. After three months, Rupert could not manage without her. Inevitably they were married. This fourth marriage was supremely happy. His book *The Arms of Time*,[55] is dedicated to June The Angel in The House.

[55] *The Arms Of Time*, published by Hamish Hamilton, 1979

Chapter 16

Creative Work

After returning from the PEN Conference in 1956, I received a post-card from Rupert Hart-Davies. It was a beauty, of a fox crouching in snow. This fox had become his insignia. As I looked at it I recalled what a poet had said: "When I'm short of an idea for a poem, I go into a pub, drink several gins, and pick up threads of talk. I can usually pull out one for a first line."

Well, I thought, I've not had any gin, but why can't I write a poem about this fox? And so it began: *Twenty years ago I saw the fox gliding along the edge of prickling corn.*

Whereupon the poem took hold of me and made me write it. In truth, it unrolled spontaneously, and, to my surprise, if publication is anything to go by, *The Fox* became one of the most successful poems I've ever written.[56] It was broadcast more than a few times and appeared in several anthologies.

This experience recalls the words of the Irish poet, James Stephens: "I never think it would be a fine idea to sit down and write a poem.[57] No! The pome [as he pronounced it] gets hold

---

[56] 'The Fox' in *The Buttercup Children*, published by Hart-Davis, 1958.
[57] James Stephens, Irish novelist, poet, 1880-1950.

of me by the scruff of the neck and makes me sit down and write it!" It was like that with *The Fox* – after I'd written the first line. The spark, the few words that ignite a poem, took hold. Intellect takes over in the second stage of self-criticism and revision.

Many poets today read too much contemporary and experimental verse, and too little of the classics. A practice deplored by Yeats who said: "Too much reading of contemporary verse is bad.[58] A poet should soak himself in the work of the Great Masters till it becomes an unconscious background of his mind." I believe the key word is unconscious.

I'm fascinated by different poets' definition of their art which is also a craft. Edith Sitwell said simply: "Poetry is magic."[59] One of my favourites comes from Newbolt: "Poetry is a transfiguration of life heightened by the homesickness of the spirit for a perfect world."[60] and as Shelley put it: "We learn in suffering what we teach in song."[61]

This last recalls Herbert Palmer's comment on a very good poet whose descriptions of natural beauty, paintings and people were outstanding while depth of passion was missing. "She never quite touched me on the quick," he said. "Why is it? What's wrong?" I asked. His answer was immediate; "She's never suffered." It's true that suffering, lightly accepted, can be a creative experience. Many, if not most great artists' work attests to this – musicians may go deaf, such as Beethoven and Fauré, some painters may suffer defective eyesight: some attribute Turner's wonderful seas and skies to failing eyesight. Latterly he saw as through a mist. For a contented person – and how many are there? – it is sufficient simply to be.

[58] William Butler Yeats, Irish poet, 1865-1939.
[59] Edith Sitwell, British poet and critic, 1886-1964.
[60] Sir Henry John Newbolt, British poet, 1862-1938.
[61] Percy Bysshe Shelley, British poet, 1792-1822.

Dr. Arthur Rayner (aka 'The Man Who Broke The Bank at Monte
Carlo') with his new wife May on their honeymoon.
Llandudno, May 1939.

Richard circa 1947.

Catherine aged 3 years, 1953.

William Aubrey Martin Hesketh. Aged 53, 1960.

Fisher House garden, July 1967.
Phoebe with kitty 'Tansy'
Grandsons Julian (left) Francis (right)
Martin, Jutta,
Aubrey.

Phoebe Hesketh, circa 1985.

Phoebe with her granddaughter Clara aged 1 year, August 1986.

Phoebe with her grandchildren: Lindsay 5 years, Clara 7 years.
Meadow Brook Drive, Andover, June 1992.

Phoebe outside the Longfellow House.
Cambridge, Massachusetts, June 1994.

Phoebe Hesketh, 1994.

It is difficult to believe that the crystal life-giving music of Mozart came from someone so often ill, in trouble with debts and women and who lived mostly on the sharp edge of existence. But he lived in two worlds. I forget of which symphony he wrote: "I heard the whole thing in my mind before setting down a note." In the same way Wordsworth composed his *Lines Written Above Tintern Abbey*.[62] He describes how, as he walked along the banks of the Wye he wrote the whole poem in his head before reaching home an hour and twenty minutes later. Many poets recall how a line, even a few words, seems to float into their heads to become the nucleus of a poem. Certainly this is how Siegfried Sassoon wrote his much anthologised *Everyone Sang*.[63] [64]

Goethe said: "The best in man is formless.[65] I believe everything genius does, as genius, happens unconsciously. Man cannot stay long in the conscious state; he has to plunge back into the unconscious for that is where his living roots are."

Rilke substantiates this in his Letters when he writes about Cézanne – that before 'it has never been demonstrated to what extent painting goes on of its own accord among the colours, how much they must be left entirely alone to explain each other, their intercourse between themselves, that is the essence of painting. Anyone who interrupts or arranges, who lets his human notions, his wit, his advocacy, his intellectual agility anywhere enter into the action, disturbs and obscures the function of the colours." [66] [67]

Because direct, personal experience carries weight I quote a small example of my own. I was in bed one night when two

[62] William Wordsworth, major British poet, 1770-1850.
[63] Siegfried Sassoon, British poet, writer and soldier, 1886-1967.
[64] 'Everyone Sang' in *Collected Poems* published by Faber and Faber, 1961.
[65] Johann Wolfgang von Goethe, German writer, statesman, 1749-1832.
[66] Rainer Maria Rilke, Austrian poet, novelist, 1875-1926.
[67] Paul Cézanne, French artist, 1839-1906.

145

g

lines, unasked for or thought of, floated into my mind: *I am alone in a bright field drifting towards a closing gate. . .* at which point I fell asleep. Next morning I awoke with the completed poem:

> *The gap narrows and I reach for the latch*
> *but the black stallion arches through*
> *trampling pale hems of dreams*

and onward to the end, almost without my volition.[68]

But poems rarely come like this. It might be argued that poems are not made but given. It's usually a bit of both. I wrote the title poem of *Prayer for Sun* in my head in the car while my husband drove to Ludlow and back two or three times to take Catherine out from school. It was a true story beginning with my urgent desire for light, obscured by two trees, outside our bedroom window. The poem tells of the unfeeling landlord's refusal at which I did, literally, pray for the removal of the trees. For twelve years I continued willing it to be so. Then one night a terrific storm of thunder and lightning, of which I heard nothing, arose. Next morning I awoke to a new strength of light through the curtains. Wondering, I got up and drew them aside. To my amazement, below me on the garden path lay the huge white beam which had obscured the sun, and tapped on the wall, lying full length on the path. The last leaves, for it was autumn, blinded the fanlight above the front door.

I rang up the landlord: "Come and remove the tree which for twelve years has been stealing our light!" The following spring, the large rowan which stood beside the white beam, developed a disease and died. The man who carted it away said, as he climbed into the wagon, "You must be a witch," and smiling he tossed me a bare twig.

[68] Extract from 'The Horses' in *Preparing To Leave*, published by Enitharmon, 1977.

By this time my friend and mentor, Herbert Palmer, had died as he would have wished, of a stroke. His last words: "It's taken my writing hand and my fishing arm," said it all.

We had often worked together at a poem; I had suggested alterations to his *The Old Knight*, title poem of a collection published in 1949.[69] This I read at his memorial service in St Albans in 1961:

> *Think not of me as old and grey*
> *With rusted helm and broken shield,*
> *But turn your mind to yesterday*
> *When I rode shining down the field.*

On the credit side of the sad year, I had a happy relationship with John Barron Mays whom I'd met shortly after Richard's death.[70] Here was a poet who never received due recognition. Perhaps this was because of his other attainments. I first met him while giving a reading in Liverpool at which he was chairman. He was then a social worker mainly concerned with boys' clubs, living in Nile Street, a deprived part of Liverpool. This was sometime in the late 1940s. Later in 1953, he sent me his first poems which were full of vivid descriptions of places, people and the countryside. Probably he lacked the confidence to publicise his poetry and anyhow he worked too hard. Soon he became a lecturer, and later held the Chair of Social Science at Liverpool University. His books on juvenile crime were not only well-known, but recognised reading for students: *Growing Up in a City*, *The Young Pretenders*, *Crime and the Social Structure*. These books were intensely readable and authoritative. By this time he had married the admirable Angela who completely understood his gloomy moods and often teased him out of pessimism. Several years younger, full

---

[69] Extract from *The Old Knight, A poem sequence for the present times*, published by Dent, 1949.

[70] John Barron Mays, poet, author, sociology professor, 1914–1987.

of guts and enterprise, Angela cared for all his needs. A social worker herself, she also shared his interests, and bore him two children. No doubt his success was largely due to her. They bought a cottage in Willaston and later moved to an imposing house and garden on the west of Chester.

I have Angela to thank for some of the happiest weekends of my life both during and after my marriage. John and I were free to spend hours, days, together, walking beside the Dee, tramping the country and having lunch at wayside pubs where we discussed life and poetry, and dissected each other's poems.

For seven years, during this period, John was on the panel in BBC Radio Four's *Round Britain Quiz*. No one would have guessed the intellectual quality hidden under his quiet manner. A depressive, he was an intensely private person. Depth of feeling and passion surfaced only in his poetry. As he wrote in *The Gift of Blood*.[71]

> *I need my aloneness. I need*
> *A road that has no traffic taking*
> *Mind to horizons, thoughts to sea.*

This total lack of showmanship, occasionally austere manner, meant that he was often misjudged. I introduced him to Frank Singleton (my former mentor – Editor of the Bolton newspaper), thinking that the two intellectuals would harmonise. I couldn't have been more wrong: instantly they disliked one another. John seemed to shrivel into a shell before Frank's ebullience and extroversion. Whereas Frank's reaction later voiced, was "That man won't do," John felt damped and crushed by Frank's confidence and enthusiasm. "He's a total extrovert," was his only comment. Again this encounter showed how, contrary to general opinion, two opposites do not make a good partnership. I felt far more in sympathy with John's Hardyesque view of life's ultimate tragedy, how

[71] From *The Gift of Blood*, a selection of poems published by Enitharmon, 1981.

everything comes to an end; however joyful the union of two lovers, one is left with loneliness and grief. How the declining years of many – if not most – people are shadowed by some sort of disability at best, of waning powers and loss of friends. We both found it difficult, false even, to "Eat, drink and be merry for tomorrow we die."

I believe the majority of poets are manic depressives, but John was seldom in the manic state. Although on occasions he greatly enjoyed good wine and food. Then he would expand with his natural flowering of wit.

We did several courses together on Creative Writing and Poetry at Adult colleges of Education. He was an excellent reader who made both his and my poems come alive. My poems sounded better than they were! I remember one occasion, at the Lancashire College at Chorley, when we played tapes of three contemporary poets; R. S. Thomas, Charles Causley and Philip Larkin. The first two, especially Causley with his bracing ballads, were very well received, as were the first few of Larkin's. Unfortunately, we hadn't played this tape beforehand, and half way through came a poem in which the poet had to get out of bed to "have a piss." Then followed a few fucks and such like words. It was impossible to stop the tape without looking foolish; we sat it out to the shocked and pained silence of a group of middle-class, middle-aged, grey-haired ladies.

The great thing about our friendship was the total relaxation in each other's company. No need to talk, no demands or strain. We were free, as in the rarest of marriages. Later I grew to realise that the happiest and most enduring friendships I've had with men were with those who were not lovers or would-be lovers. As C. S. Lewis points out in *The Four Loves* the best of these is friendship which, if it occurs in marriage, is the happiest one of all.[72][73]

[72] Clive Staples Lewis, British novelist, poet and academic, 1898–1963.
[73] *The Four Loves*, Published by Geoffrey Bles, 1960.

The last time I saw John, in the Lakes, in the late 1970s, he wasn't well, complaining of fatigue and depression. He was then in his 60s: I thought it was a temporary malaise. But no, it was the start of a long drawn out, painful, fatal illness – leukaemia. Angela was indeed his ministering angel, visiting him in Clatterbridge Hospital for hours, days, weeks and when, at the end, there was barely room for yet another blood transfusion needle, she helped the nurses with his care. During this period he refused to see me and, indeed, any of his close friends, perhaps to avoid spoiling our last meetings by distress at his condition. I did once manage to fix a day for a final visit, but at the last moment Angela rang to say he was unfit to see anyone.

His fourth collection of poems *The Gift of Blood* was written before he realised the truth of his illness. How I miss him! Not merely for collaboration over poems, but for the exchange of visits; many times he came here, and many times we tramped the moors discussing, not only poetry, but "shoes and ships and sealing-wax". Of all my friends he has left the biggest gap in my life.

Chapter 17

Poetry and Poets

During one of my poetry readings I was asked a common, unanswerable question – "Why, and how, do you write poetry?" Taken aback, I could only reply: "I really can't tell you. It seems to come out sideways when I'm not thinking!" Robert Frost said: "You cannot write a poem by taking thought."[74] Whenever I've wanted to write a poem and made a conscious effort to do so, it has come to nothing. A friend of mine, a poet, said that while working at one poem, another came nudging into her mind, so that the first one had to be abandoned.

Another stimulus is actually being asked for a poem. However one may brush aside this request, it remains in the mind. For example, in 1973, I was asked to submit a collection of verse suitable for young people. I replied that I never wrote verse for children, but I might find several poems that they could enjoy. The result was *A Song of Sunlight* published in 1974. Only about two poems were written specifically for this collection.

As previously mentioned, one of my most successful books *Preparing To Leave* was published in 1977. Following this,

[74] Robert Frost, American poet, 1874-1963.

The Eighth Day: Selected Poems was published in 1980. Although well reviewed, this book was not as successful as its predecessor. I believe the inclusion of my poems from 1948, which many people prefer to the later ones, had little appeal for contemporary critics who look for intellectual subtlety – often a synonym for obscurity – recondite allusions, and abandonment of form. They discount much genuine verse written from the depth of being in preference to that hammered out by the top half of the brain. Wordsworth's dictum: "The purpose of poetry is to give pleasure" is reversed to the point of alienating many intelligent, literary and sensitive members of the public. Fred Beake writes: "Established forms must be sacrificed to a bogus originality."[75]

I remember C. S. Lewis summing up: "Modern poetry is new in a new way, in that it cannot be remembered." True originality lies in giving new expression to the time-worn and unchangeable by unusual juxtaposition of words, words used in new relationships. For example:

> *Jewels five words long*
> *That on stretched forefinger of Old Time*
> *Sparkle for ever* [76]

The much maligned Tennyson has a great deal to give to contemporary writers. And Tennyson, my first love and passion, gave me my allegiance, to music in poetry – the sort of poetry which, being memorable, beats through the blood with the rhythms of life itself, and sings to the brain in old age when much that is trivial or forced has long since run through the sieve of time.

There was another reason for my devotion to Tennyson – the

[75] Fred Beake, British poet born 1948.
[76] From *The Princess* by Alfred Lord Tennyson, first published by Moxon, London, 1847.

152

English teacher at my first boarding-school, whose enthusiasm for the poet shone through her and reflected, if not on the whole class, at least on me. She so splendidly brought to life both Tennyson and Greek history with its legends, philosophy and the Trojan War. When the two subjects came together my delight was doubled. The poem *Oenone* still gives me intense pleasure seventy years on.[77] To colour drab moments I find myself repeating it, and in moments of reflection, these lines have often floated into my head:

> For now the noonday quiet holds the hill;
>   The grasshopper is silent in the grass,
>   The lizard, with his shadow on the stone.
> Rests like a shadow and the winds are dead.
> The purple flower droops: the golden bee
>   Is lily-cradled: I alone awake.

"Unfashionable romantic stuff of nature," the 'moderns' might scoff. This small 'coterie' exchange hidden meanings under esoteric symbols, and clever verbalising to baffle a general audience and would-be readers. But many potential followers are shut out from their world. One critic, who is also a poet, remarked that true originality lies in the ability to use old forms and subject matter in such a way as to shine fresh light on the subject. The true poet enables you to see the ordinary afresh. Gerard Manley Hopkins said: "Poetry heightens the commonplace."[78] Obviously in a high-tech world, poets must reflect a changing environment. This is often achieved with the thrust and vitality of humour, successfully done by Roger McGough in *Let Me Die A Young Man's Death*.[79][80] This poem has delighted many members of my Creative Writing classes.

[77] *Oenone*, from *Poems*, published by Moxon, London, 1833.
[78] Gerard Manley Hopkins, British poet, 1844-1899.
[79] Roger Joseph McGough, British poet, writer and broadcaster. Born 1937.
[80] From *The Mersey Sound* an anthology published by Penguin, 1967.

At this point I should affirm that all poetry can be described as verse in a general way, but not all verse is poetry. Dividing lines are very fine. Lewis Carroll, Edward Lear, Ogden Nash and others so enliven us with vitality, originality and wit that they seem to straddle the boundary line. Lewis Carroll's[81] *The Walrus and the Carpenter* and other rhymes survive in this way:[82]

> *The Walrus and the Carpenter*
> *Were walking close at hand;*
> *They wept like anything to see*
> *Such quantities of sand*
> *'If this were only cleared away,'*
> *They said, 'it would be grand!'*
>
> *'If seven maids with seven mops*
> *Swept it for half a year,*
> *Do you suppose' the Walrus said.*
> *'That they could get it clear?'*
> *'I doubt it' said the carpenter,*
> *And shed a bitter tear.*

A poet who combines wit, humour and genuine poetry – the occasional magic touch – which distinguishes it from verse is Charles Causley.[83] Master of the ballad form, his verse is memorable. Causley's *The Ballad of Charlotte Dymond*, is verse shot through with poetry's magic.[84] Charlotte is a young domestic servant murdered by her lover, a crippled farm-hand who cut her throat with a razor, and left her lying in a bog on Bodmin Moor. This compelling story written, presumably, from a newspaper cutting, is related with verve and tenderness.

[81] Lewis Carroll, British writer, 1832-1898.
[82] Published in *Through The Looking Glass*, Macmillan, 1871.
[83] Charles Stanley Causley, British poet and writer, 1917-2003.
[84] *The Ballad of Charlotte Dymond*, published by Dartington Hall. C. Eric McNally, 1958.

It illustrates how true stories can fire the imagination into poetry. The inspiration for two of my poems: *The Meths Men* and *More Than Grass* sprang from newspaper articles.[85][86]

I mentioned my poem *Prayer for Sun* in an earlier chapter.[87] This turned out to be one of the most successful 'ballady' poems. It took over a year to write and frequently haunted my dreams. It concerns my previously mentioned battle with Liverpool Water Authority to allow us to cut down two trees which entirely obscured the light from our lovely Fisher House.

Prayer For Sun

Two trees outside my window stood;
I might have lived in the middle of a wood
For all I saw of the sun – the light
Flowed into a rowan's beaded head
To glaze the berries paint-box red
Or raise new blossom whiter than bread,
But the sun was hidden from sight.

Leaf-locked with the rowan a whitebeam pressed
Against my window; blinded the west;
Scratched the pane when I lay there ill;
Trickled with rain down my window-sill.
Visitors said: 'What a friendly tree!'
Of my faithful enemy.
At Candlemas, down on my knees,
I begged the landlord to fell the trees:
'One drinks the morning light away;
One drains the evening dregs. Midday,
Midnight are laced in grave-green gloom.
I must have the sun in my room!'

[85] From *Preparing To Leave*, published by Enitharmon, 1977.
[86] From *Prayer For Sun*, published by Hart-Davis, 1966.
[87] *Prayer For Sun*, published by Hart-Davis, 1966.

The landlord laughed; his bowler-hat
Was as hard as his look; his answer flat
As a paving-stone: 'I must have rain.
Trees attract it. Don't ask again,
Remember you live on a watershed
By courtesy,' he curtly said.

I watched the trees grow big with dark,
Opened the window, touched each bark –
Whitebeam with left hand, rowan with right,
And prayed for light.

I lay in my leaf-green grave again;
Two trees grew tall behind my brain,
Darkened my dreams with leaves and rain.
Lost in a house in a wood I wept:
'Lord, pluck this whitebeam from my eye,
This rowan that blocks the morning sky.'
I heard the thunder of God's reply,
Yet still I slept –
'Gather their branches one by one;
Twist their roots – if rain or sun
May ever by prayer be won!'

I woke. The visiting day was white
As a stranger stripped before me: Light.
I zipped the curtains back; the sky
Dazzled the window, drew my eye
From where it sought to where it found
A light-flash later – on the ground.

Was I awake or rocked in dream?
With leaves hair-locked in the garden gate,
Below me shivered the tough whitebeam
Felled by the axe of Fate.
One pang was drowned in murderous joy –

Whose was the hand strong to destroy
This more-than-human tree?
The storm was God's but it broke through me.

The landlord swore at God's will done
In a tree that wrestled the wind and won
My case for the sun.
Alone, the rowan tapped window and wall
Tossing its sun-embroidered shawl
On the empty air
Till the camp-fire coloured beads burned down
And emerald leaves shrank nutmeg-brown
From branches skeleton-bare.

Like bones they rattled the wind and cold,
Grew black as I grew bold
To summon the landlord once again:
'Your rowan will bring down no more rain!'

They called me a witch; dragged it away;
Carted the rowan, bald and grey,
Tossed me a twig for the evil done
And left me to live – and die – with the sun.

Chapter 18

Downhill All the Way

Turning to family matters, it was during the early 1960s that my father's exceptional stamina began to fail. As a pioneer in the field of radiology, he realised sadly that he was slowing down. In July 1954, aged 82 he gave, unaided, the last barium meal and X-ray for duodenal ulcer; and also developed the plates. By now he had no assistant radiographer, only a rather inexperienced secretary. Naturally, during latter years, his work had been falling off.

Inevitable retirement after such a crowded and demanding lifework was more than merely painful. His two loves, reading and the countryside, though still possible, lost edge and enjoyment once he was free from the pressure of work. His second marriage to May, thirty-seven years younger than himself, was by no means easy. Even though she'd been a cafe waitress when he married her in 1939, she had never taken responsibility. Her hard-working mother had spoiled and protected her, and my father did the same, shielding her from every difficulty and decision. Not only in their ages was the gap apparent but they were of different social backgrounds and religion – three of the main stumbling-blocks, my father had maintained, to successful marriage. Now they were thrown together whereas previously they'd been free to spend enough time apart for necessary personal space, one reason why retirement years can be more difficult than those of the earlier periods of marriage.

To begin with, things went comparatively smoothly. May learned to drive and was able to take my father for country expeditions and holidays – to Grange, the Lakes, and his favourite Llandudno. This last became a festering point in their relationship. "I'm fed up with Llandudno!" May complained on his retirement. "Now you're not tied to your miserable fortnight a year, you might take me abroad – I want to go to Spain or Greece, and I'd like a taste of Monte Carlo!" My father demurred that he was too old and tired, after over 60 years of gruelling work, to undertake foreign travel. A fierce argument ensued, but he stuck to his point. At this, May lost her temper and rushed inside from the garden in which they were sitting. Suddenly the window above his seat was pushed wide open, and the heavy Catholic Bible, which he'd given her for Christmas, was flung hard at his nearly bald head.

Like a lamb he submitted to her tantrums. How differently he'd treated my mother who never dared to have tantrums. So it was galling for me to be told, after I'd arranged to go over there for tea, "Remember, be nice to May," urged my father. "Praise her and encourage her – you know she's not used to our sort of life." Not only had I to be 'nice', but was made to feel obliged to take over the tea, sandwiches and cake, lest May, the ex-waitress, should feel put on.

She, on the other hand, had some occasions for complaint, as when Harold, my father's youngest brother, aged 77, decided to come home after sixty years in Canada. He'd worked up a successful grain business in Toronto, and had fathered two sons, of whom Herbert, the elder, became Chief of Staff, Canadian Navy and Vice-Admiral with a distinguished

159

war record. May complained that Harold clacked his false teeth and spread jam on his cake and other habits she disliked. One day after lunch he decided to have a rest on his bed. When, by tea time, he had not appeared, May went upstairs to wake him but she did not succeed; Harold was dead.

And so the family black sheep who'd been deported at the age of 16 by his distraught father, after he'd absconded from every school and been declared, by the Captain of the training ship *Conway*, as unmanageable, had returned to the fold. "Strange," said my father, "some instinct must have prompted him to come home to die."

Slowly, inexorably, my father's mind began to give way. One morning he arose at five o'clock, went out and hammered at the tobacconist's door demanding his favourite cigars. And when Elaine came to stay to relieve May, he went for her, his daughter, with steel blue eyes flashing angry sparks:

"Get out of my house!" he shouted. "I'll not have any loose women around here!" Elaine was terrified, especially when he threatened her with a knife.

Sadly, he developed cancer of the bowel and was taken into St Joseph's Hospital, Mount Street, Preston. On July 23rd, 1963, he died at the age of eighty-five.

At the time of my father's death, I was coping with my husband Aubrey's premature senility. For a long time I had attributed his failing memory and lack of concentration to stress at work. He had seen the collapse of T.M. Hesketh and Son and its takeover by Heaton's Ltd in 1952. It was a dark day when we watched the tall black finger of the first mill chimney felled like a tree – not whole with leaves intact but collapsing like a toy into smoking rubble. This sight left us distressed and wordless. Aubrey was taken on Heaton's board of managers for a while but he felt an outsider whose opinions were given little weight; and yet, being the finest judge of raw cotton, he was retained as a

160

Director of the British Cotton Growers' Association for a few more years.

Alas his diminishing grasp of events and changes gradually became more apparent; though to me, it was a temporary condition which, once he was free of responsibilities, would improve. I realised that it was useless to give him a shopping list. It was too much to expect him to consult it before coming home from the office. I used to ring up his secretary, asking her to remind him – even of one item before his return. But the ice cream or the bottle of sherry was hardly ever remembered. I teased him: "Every time I open my mouth, you shut your ears!" In fact I began to feel I was too demanding. But losing and forgetting things on such a scale led to irritation on my part and distress on his.

Eventually, when he was about 57, which would make it 1963, I took him to a psychiatrist. When I heard the verdict: 'Premature senility,' it seemed the bottom of my life had fallen out. And then, "It's a progressive condition, no chance of remission." When I asked how long I could care for him, alone, at home, he replied: "About five years is the average."

One is apt to disregard unwelcome verdicts. For the next ten years it was a constant struggle to avoid the fatal day when I could no longer cope with the situation. Among other activities, I encouraged Aubrey to keep a daily diary. At first this was easy; in fact he was still officially at work with the firm who kept him on because of his character, his ability to get on with and charm potential customers, and of his expert judgment of raw cotton. Gradually his condition worsened. The diary was written, with help, using fat coloured pencils. I tried constructive toys – putting pegs into holes, making patterns with counters, and so on. I took him to rug-making classes, but the teacher gave him up. Listening to music was about the only thing he could do – with delight and understanding, for he was intensely musical. And one outdoor

161

task he enjoyed – cutting logs, and collecting wood. He would wander into nearby fields and coppices, happy as the schoolboy he had become. Only after he'd lost three handsaws did I give up. Then he'd simply wander away – sometimes, to my consternation, on his bicycle – which led to telephone calls asking if I knew an elderly gentleman in a green anorak.

The next experiment was a health farm where he had spiritual healing. This relaxed him from growing tension. Along with an excellent diet, walks in beautiful grounds, recitals of music, outings in the car, he really seemed to improve. And I began, again, to hope.

After this he saw a neurologist in Manchester who took him into hospital for a brain scan and lumbar puncture, which upset him, as it upset me, so I counted this last move as a total failure.

At this time he was attending a hospital psychiatric department for occupational therapy. The teacher grew to love him, he responded to her understanding. The most trying part of this period was waiting for the ambulance to call in the mornings. Sometimes he'd be ready and waiting for two hours. If I took him in by car, they'd be annoyed at having called in vain, and I never knew what time he'd be back home.

By now, he sometimes got up in the night and was so restless that he slept in another room. On one occasion he burst into my room at 4 a.m. wearing his hunting jacket and bowler hat, brandishing a crop: "Come on, get up! Get up! It's time to be off!" The whole situation was so distressing and hopeless that I began to feel considerable strain. And to my shame, I often lost my temper, which made matters worse. Of course, I bitterly regretted it, and assuring him I loved him, asked for his forgiveness. He was a lovely man, and how he must have suffered! And how painful were those glimpses of his normal self. After some stressful episode he would say: "I must go to some place!" realising that the position at home was becoming untenable.

Though a kindly woman came in two or three times a week to help, it was little enough. I needed someone, preferably a relative, living in. My daughter Catherine was working and came home to help on some weekends. My son Martin had him to stay an occasional weekend, but he saw the best side of it, and was helped considerably by Jutta, his wife. Aubrey, with his inherent kindness and courtesy, was able to adjust wonderfully to a new situation involving people he knew.

As time went on he became incontinent, and though I got him up in the night, there was, often enough, a wet bed in the morning. One day I'd got him ready for hospital – all clean on – when, at the last moment, he was soaked. And then it was I lost my temper. I knew this was inexcusable, and the memory of my behaviour, as I write this, gives me not only a feeling of remorse, but acute pain. I can only hope that, where ever he is, he forgives me. Looking back, I believe he would have forgiven my various peccadilloes which, had I confided in him and trusted sufficiently in his love and goodness, would have spared us both much suffering.

Eventually, at the insistence of doctors, social workers and his own two sisters, I reluctantly agreed for him to go into a psycho-geriatric hospital. Here the sisters and nurses were not only extremely kind but, recognising his rare qualities, treated him as he deserved. He had full range of the garden, and was allowed out for daily walks with a patient suffering from a temporary breakdown. I had him home every weekend, and took him out mid-week. In fact, he was happier than I had dared hope. Yet at home I missed him terribly, and felt I was shirking my duty.

All went well for a year or so and then he became confused and agitated. He was given higher doses of a tranquilliser to my dismay. But my protestations were of no avail; he was out of my hands. Yet even on his cloudiest days, his face would light up when he saw me – and this cut me more than anything else, feeling I had betrayed him, and was helpless to help. But when he came home – now only for days – I would take him back smart and clean. In fact, one day he strayed into a committee meeting of the hospital management committee and, chatting with his usual courtesy, smiling and agreeing with them, he was mistaken for the new doctor until a nurse appeared: "I think you've got one of our patients in here with you!"

It was those sudden clear periods, amid the cloudiness, that I found most distressing. Towards the end of 1975 I begged permission to have him home for Christmas. A few days later he had a stroke – a severe one. I drove up one morning outside his bedroom window, and my heart missed a beat. I saw him thrashing about in the bed. After that he never knew me. I brought Catherine home from college and for a time we watched by his bed. The doctor arrived and said Aubrey would never recognise us again, and advised us to return home. We became more and more upset and, thinking that this might go on for some time, I took the doctor's advice and drove home. Less than an hour later a nurse rang to say Aubrey was dead. It was January 4th, 1976.

Chapter 19

Widowhood

As I write in March 1993, it's hard to believe that Aubrey's decline began over 30 years ago. It seems to belong to another life lived by another person. Buddha maintained there is no such thing as a stable personality. Every seven years we change, and are changed. The baby is different from the toddler; and the teenager is barely, if at all, recognisable as the three-year-old.

Not only the passing years change us, we are changed by experience, mainly through the people we have met on the journey. How much the essential 'I' – irrespective of external happenings – changes us, is impossible to say. This is where heredity overrides environment and circumstance. A misty area, it may be that the 'I', the unique one, attracts to itself the very circumstances that shape, and re-shape, it.

I'm sure the gradual mental deterioration of the man I married, the demands made on me, and my response to these demands, have changed me – though not at the time of re-shaping. How regrettable that so often it takes the loss of someone to realise how much that person has meant, and to realise one's lack of understanding, compassion, and gratitude. The pains of regret are terrible, of remorse even more destructive. Loneliness and emptiness hammered into me the truth of how much I loved him. Always I had recognised him as the 'better' person. There was something wholly clear and pure in his nature. To the end he remained unsullied by the dark influences of the world. He fought his way through business competition with its tangles of self-interest and deceit and was exploited and manipulated. All these thoughts came crowding in to intensify my misery.

With husband dead and children gone, you are no longer the centre of anyone's life. In fact, you are no longer needed, to the point of losing identity. Succumbing to this feeling reduces you to a mechanism, an automaton who gets up every morning, performs the necessary repetitive tasks, while wishing it would all end.

Soon after Aubrey's death I moved from our rambling old home into a modern bungalow. Lovely as it was, Fisher House had become impossible to manage on my own. It wasn't easy because I left my beloved house in Rivington with its friendly community and people I knew so well. Rooted there after 45 years and a family life, I felt like a torn up plant. At first there was much to do, putting the house in order, and finding a gardener to tend the large garden. But the loneliness was ever present.

As after the loss of Richard, I tried to turn myself into a sort of cabbage, to anaesthetise my 'feeling' self. It is a way of protecting from despair, and has the virtue of submerging the ego, and becoming a minute part of the universe. I have frequently heard people say: "Loneliness is a terrible thing!" Often, in protective garment, you may sail through the waters of everyday. Then the shock of some simple happening jerks you back into your true self. One October evening I came home to my bungalow with the earth smelling of damp leaves which was in itself nostalgic enough. The added smell of wood smoke from a bonfire recalled all the bonfires we had lit together and I was overcome. It was the first time I had wept since Aubrey's death.

The worst thing that can happen to widows is to indulge in self-pity, which sends even the kindest friends away. People will listen with real sympathy for about three months. I fought against this, and set out cultivating a new life.

Aubrey's illness inevitably brought stress and strain but surprisingly this didn't inhibit my creative work. In fact, I'd say that conflict, deprivation, and frustration are the best soil for the flowering of the creative spirit. I can't speak personally for painting and musical composition, but I do know I wrote then, as many, and often better, poems than I'd written before. Perhaps they were what readers described as 'sadder', but, stripped of excesses, they were sparer, and therefore stronger.

A collection of my poems aptly named *Preparing To Leave* was published in 1977. Most fortunately it had an excellent review in *The Times Literary Supplement* with the result that the book was sold out within six months. The success of this publication led to requests for poetry readings which put meaning and purpose into what threatened to become a barren old age.

There were readings, classes and creative writing groups ahead. I had already given a series of classes which included English Literature, Poetry, and also subjects varying from the Environment, Comparative Religion and Current Affairs. These sessions led to lively and lengthy discussions. This venture still stands out as a highlight of my life. Every member of the group was lively-minded, intelligent, and enthusiastic, so that I received back far more than I gave.

Many years have passed since my creative writing classes so I was amazed when recently stopped by a woman who asked, "Excuse me, but can you be Phoebe Hesketh?" She went on to enlarge on her enjoyment and remembrance of those classes.

Widowhood is a great testing time. Either one sinks under the huge demands of making a new life, cultivating friends and interests, or gradually one adjusts. The important period is the waiting, with hope. It is impossible to become a different person, with renewed vision, in a few months. There must be a period of hibernation, allowing the subconscious to come to the rescue. This depends, largely, on health, age, and chance or luck. It seems that new friends enter one's life and open doors undreamed of.

I was fortunate. Because I'd published both poetry and prose, several people, unknown to me, wrote friendly letters – often sending samples of their own writing, or asking me to give advice, or to address their pet societies. There were official requests for readings, broadcasts and poems for anthologies – mostly for schools and young people. I rather regretfully wrote myself down as a 'Children's Poet'. To cheer myself I recall the words of C.S. Lewis: "A writer who cannot write what children enjoy is no good!" Small comfort perhaps in an age when poets accepted and praised by the critics are those who write for the 'inner circle' of reviewers and editors of poetry magazines. Their work is recondite, intellectual, and to quote an old friend: ". . .written with the top half of the brain – no spiritual light in it." Slowly I moved on to the next and entirely different phase of my life.

Chapter 20

New Ventures

Turning again to family matters, our daughter Catherine revealed unexpected determination. As mentioned in a previous chapter, she left boarding school at the age of 16 and returned home to complete her education at a local college. In 1971 Catherine obtained a diploma in Institutional Management and thereafter followed a succession of 'hard grind' jobs in the food service industry. Long hours, unremitting toil, and exacting requirements took their toll on her. One day she announced: "It's time for a change. I'm going for a Diploma in Nutrition and Dietetics." At this news her former headmistress exclaimed: "Do dissuade Catherine from this. It's a highly scientific course, and she has no more science than Biology. She'll never make it."

In vain I pleaded but her mind was made up. She undertook the two year course in the company of students with advanced science degrees. It seemed an impossible venture. But Catherine literally incarcerated herself and worked round the clock. She passed her exams by a hair's breadth. This was followed by six months' clinical training and to our amazement she did extremely well. This was probably due to her success in inspiring patients to follow required diets.

h

After working at a hospital in Manchester, she decided, to my dismay, to leave and follow her future husband Derek to Limerick in South West Ireland. He had found a job with a microelectronics company based in the USA. One morning in 1977, the year after Aubrey's death, she rang with the news of her decision. I had never been so hatefully surprised. "But you can't do this. . ." I began. "I'm sorry Mum," she replied, "but I've got to do it!"

There comes a day when children are no longer dependant on parents; a sadder one when parents are dependant on children. This day, I realised, had come. With Aubrey gone, Martin and his family preoccupied, I had come to rely on Catherine for emotional response and she in turn had felt the need to free herself. When she left in January 1978, I was devastated.

Having settled into their new home, Catherine opened a small private dietetic practice in Limerick, but it was not enough. There was no Dietetic Department in the Regional Hospital so she made an appointment with the senior consultant physician. "Other major hospitals employ dietitians," she said. "Surely you need a dietitian here in Limerick. Perhaps I can fill that need!" The doctor, taken aback, exclaimed: "Well! You're certainly a determined young lady!"

After seeing her credentials he decided to let her go ahead and work a few hours each week. Soon she was working full time as the department grew and many patients were referred for dietetic treatment and counselling. So began a happy and successful period. Catherine was well thought of by doctors, patients and nurses alike.

During the next eight years I made at least twenty flights to visit Catherine and Derek in their bungalow in County Limerick. Their home was situated on the verge of attractive countryside with uplifting mountain views. Before leaving the old world of home, Ireland seemed to me to be a far older world, of myths and legends, pixies and fairies. I was not to be disappointed and went, with Catherine, on some magical trips.

In recent years, the city of Limerick has become a vibrant, thriving hub with a prestigious university. It is a far cry from the grey dusty days of the seventies when litter was piled high in gutters and roadways. I recall many traffic jams. On one occasion Catherine's car was stopped in a main street by a car whose driver was so inured to waiting, that he was reading a newspaper and smoking a cigar at the wheel. However, the city is graced by the wide slow-flowing River Shannon and the clean grey Cathedral of St Mary, impressive on its bank. I used to gaze with delight at this scene, especially when stone and water shone gold in the evening sun.

Driving out of town along the country lanes can be hazardous. Apart from the narrow winding roads, the drivers tend to be unpredictable. One day, the car slowly driving along in front of us turned right without warning. There followed the screech of brakes and a minor 'bump.' "Oh my God!" Catherine exclaimed as she jumped out of the car. "Ach!" exclaimed the other driver, "But I always turn right here on a Wednesday afternoon!"

If the narrow, bumpy Irish roads lengthen the mile in a car, they sweeten it on foot. As in the Vale of Aherlow, County Tipperary, where the hedgerows threaded among the mountains are hung with honeysuckle and hooped with briar roses. Fuchsias swing crimson and purple bells above every wild flower in the book – from speedwell to star of Bethlehem. Driving home on a summer evening between curd-white crowns of elder and regiments of six-foot high hogweed in flower, the air goes to your head. To the left is a field of cows fetlock-deep in yellow flags, to the right cottage gardens gladdened with arum lilies. In this mystic countryside where people have time to live, there's a quality of light best

171

described by Wordsworth as *The light that never was on sea or land.*

It was a sad day for me when Derek took an opportunity to move to Massachusetts where his firm was based. By now they had a delightful baby, Clara, whom I loved beyond reason. Also, I had hugely enjoyed my trips to Ireland and its magical country in the South West. I'll never forget the first sight of MacGillycuddy's Reeks. These magnificent mountains rise suddenly to view from the road, standing sharp, outlined in damson-blue against the pale horizon – almost like cut-outs from a stage fairy story.

How well I remember our journeys through the countryside and walks along the splendid coastline. I longed to return to the lovely Glen of Aherlow – it all comes back and haunts me still. In 1987 the news came of their pending move to the United States and I put down the telephone and wept.

Chapter 21

A Narrow Escape

During the years following Aubrey's death I had pursued a recently discovered aptitude for oil painting. Having attended a series of art classes, this hobby came to the rescue on long lonely evenings. One winter night when I had 'the black dog' on me,[88] I brought out my paints and, out of my head, painted two poppy heads in oils. It turns out that oil painting had become a form of therapy. In addition to painting, poetry readings and radio broadcasts, I took up volunteer work, travelled to foreign lands and made many new friends.

This brings to mind an evening in March 1982. I was driving home after a long walk and dinner with friends when suddenly, and most surprisingly, I opened my eyes to a white ceiling and figures in white hovering around. I might have been in heaven, for I felt feather light, lying on air. A figure stood over me and spoke: "You've broken your ankle, knee-cap, several ribs, and damaged your head." I smiled and said, "It's not true! What happened?" "You drove through a stone wall in someone's garden." The police questioned me, but I could remember nothing after saying good-bye to my friends

[88] Winston Churchill – reference to depression, 1874–1965.

outside their house. Presently a nurse put fourteen stitches in my head after which I spent six days in the Intensive Care Unit at Bolton District and General Hospital. I was regularly trundled down endless corridors for X-rays. My son Martin and his wife Jutta visited each day and invited me to stay with them after I was discharged. Many friends came. "You poor thing!" they exclaimed; "You must be in a lot of pain!" I never felt a thing. Nature's anaesthesia did a wonderful job.

When the day came to depart, I wanted to go home, but Martin and Jutta dissuaded me. "Who will look after you?" they exclaimed. As if by magic, my younger grandson Julian appeared. "I'll take you home, and look after you for a few days," he volunteered. And so he did. As we approached the house, a sudden doubt assailed me. "I've just thought, Julian, you'll have to help me undress, and take me to the bathroom, and do all!" He never turned a hair, taking my pants down with professional unconcern.

A week later, I was ensconced with Martin and Jutta, who turned their sitting-room into a downstairs bedroom, and generally cared for me. I was brought a daily breakfast-tray by my older grandson Francis who was living at home. I learned to hobble around the garden, encased in plaster from ankle to thigh, and give attention to the crocuses pushing purple, white, and gold fingers through the cold March ground.

On Good Friday April 9th, my daughter Catherine and her husband Derek arrived from Ireland to take me home. Jutta had cooked a most delicious lunch of trout and trimmings with a fruity pudding to follow. Later that afternoon, Catherine and Derek drove home and spent a week with me. Francis arrived toward the end of their stay and took care of my needs. By this time, I had become self-sufficient but how thankful I was for my family's loving care and attention. Indeed I was acutely aware of this narrow escape from a potentially fatal accident.

My poem *Journey* came to mind during the long recovery

period.[89] This poem – from a collection published in 1980 – reflects painful past recollections:

Journey

I have died many times –
every night and every morning when
I leave the unknown darkness
where most I am alive
seeing shapes and colours never seen by day.

I died with my mother and my father –
and the roof was blown off my world.

Summers and winters drifted by
Till the snow was a white cherry
Shaken outside my window.
A blackbird whistled the world awake
and my son to be born in Autumn
quickened as I stepped on the first daisies.

There was singing in the sap
that ended in his green death
playing by the river.
Then I was hollow as a wren's egg
blown by a schoolboy,
coming to life only in the green darkness
where his tent was pitched
under the willow.

One night he took my hand
telling of my journey over land and water
beginning again,
and he spoke to my daughter before birth.

[89] From *The Eighth Day,* published by Enitharmon, 1980.

Again the cherry and the blackbird,
falling leaf and snow
in magic circles
till she grew out of me –
more surely than being born –
when I'd grown into her,
made her life my own.

For that I had to suffer
a hard season of no growth
pruned low below the sunrise.
But life holds, draws, pulls
after light has gone
till the hidden flower opens
reaching for the sun.

Chapter 22

Transatlantic Travels

Following my almost fatal accident in 1982 I vowed to make the most of life and take advantage of all possible opportunities. Catherine's move from Ireland to New England in 1987 precipitated many transatlantic crossings, journeys I would never have dreamed of undertaking in my earlier years.

One hot day in June 1987, I arrived in Massachusetts to a warm welcome from Catherine and Derek. By now they had a second child Lindsay, born in April of that year. At this time the family lived in a rented house – surrounded by trees – in Tewksbury. My great enjoyment was to wander through the aromatic pine wood fringing a lake at the bottom of the hill. My footsteps softened on the pine needle carpet. I listened to many birds foreign to me, and disturbed woodchucks and raccoons to streak out of sight.

Squirrels leapt from branch to branch, and sometimes a scarlet cardinal flashed through the gloom. Standing at the edge of the lake in the warm still scented air, I seemed to be the only human being in the world. It was like stepping back in time beyond and before the sounds and smells of civilisation. It was how Longfellow must have felt when he wrote:[90]

[90] Henry Wadsworth Longfellow, poet, 1807-1882.

By the shores of Gitchie Gumee,
By the shining Big-Sea-Water
Stood the wigwam of Nokomis,
Daughter of the moon Nokomis.

Filled with exultation and true to my name, I felt like a daughter of the moon itself.[91]

One day Catherine drove me and two year old Clara to a bird sanctuary near Lake Deering in New Hampshire. The long straight road swept northwards through mile after mile of forest. I recalled the words of a man I'd met on the plane who said: "Where I live it's sixty per cent water and forty per cent forest." This is a land in which lakes and forests form the natural landscape. We picnicked on the lakeshore and watched Clara's face light up as she threw small stones into the water.

Before long Catherine and Derek bought a house in Andover, a lovely town of light bright houses, white churches, gardens and tree-bordered squares, about twenty-five miles north of Boston. As with many towns in outlying areas, the houses are built on circles or ovals. Spaced well apart, they overlook a central area of grass, trees and flowering shrubs. This is a most happy arrangement which allows privacy with communication. Moreover, a road runs round the central area – a permanent delight for children on bicycles, and safe from the main road.

Such was Meadow Brook Drive where, in Number Four, the family went to live. The house is partly mellow brick, partly sage-green shingles, two-storied with a basement family room, and stands in the usual large area of grass. This grass became Catherine's weekly penance in the summer when she charged around like Boadicea seated on a clanging motor mower. In order to enliven the monotony of grass, she built a flower bed; now a colourful addition to the scene.

[91] Extract from *The Song Of Hiawatha* by Longfellow, 1855.

Since 1987, I've flown to New England seven times. The Andover move in 1988 proved to be a really happy one, resulting in many trips and literary pilgrimages.

The first one, in 1989, was to Concord where we spent an afternoon in the Thoreau Lyceum and lingered in a replica of Henry David Thoreau's famous house in the Woods at Walden where he spent two years in semi-retirement from the world.[92] This was when his classic *Walden* was written. In the one tiny downstairs room were three chairs – "one for solitude, two for company, and three for society." Chief of his rare visitors were Ralph Waldo Emerson, poet and philosopher, and Bronson Alcott, father of Louisa May and three other talented daughters.[93][94]

Firm friends, the three men played a major role in the formation of the Transcendentalist movement, advocating the abolition of slavery, religious tolerance, and justice for the under-privileged. Thoreau himself, poet and natural scientist, though free-thinking and unorthodox, upheld Christian ideals – his classic statement in *Civil Disobedience* was the basis of Gandhi's campaign for non-violence. Not only was he a lover of nature, but an acute observer, spending hours, days, in the woods and fields. Some of his observations and questions were illustrated and pinned on the walls of the Lyceum. These I found fascinating. For instance, he asks: "How did these beautiful rainbow tints get into the shell of the freshwater clam buried deep in the mud of our dark river?"

And: "If you have built castles in the air, your work need not be lost; that is where they should be. Now put foundations under them." Here is one that particularly appeals to me: "I would rather sit in the open air; for no dust gathers on grass unless where man has broken ground." Some of these sayings

[92] Henry David Thoreau, American author, poet and philosopher, 1817-1862.
[93] Ralph Waldo Emerson, American essayist, lecturer and poet, 1803-1882.
[94] Amos Bronson Alcott, American teacher, writer and philosopher, 1799-1888.

were very likely the fruit of the three friends' conversations: "What is religion? That which is never spoken." All three men were Unitarians. Though Emerson had been ordained as a minister, he later grew out of what he felt to be too narrow and constricting.

Bronson Alcott also was highly unorthodox. For one thing, he started a school which initiated advanced methods of teaching which resulted in much public indignation. What should have caused more indignation was his impracticality and failure to properly provide for his wife and daughters. When Catherine and I visited his Concord home, Orchard House, we were made aware of this by a most excellent guide. For a time the family, growing their own fruit and vegetables, were vegans. Bronson, at one time, ran an experimental farm, Fruitlands, which probably supplied much of the meagre family diet.

Amazingly, the hard-working mother kept the family in health enough for creative work. Of the four daughters, Louisa May became the most famous with *Little Women* and subsequent novels which ultimately provided financial security for the family.[95] All free-thinkers and philanthropists, they upheld justice for all, of whatever race, and, naturally, campaigned against slavery in any form, whether in fields and factories, or in the home.

Subsequent trips to New England gave me the opportunity to visit the former homes of well-known writers and poets for whom I have the greatest admiration.

[95] Louisa May Alcott, American poet and writer, 1832-1888.

Chapter 23

New England Experiences (I)

The summer of 1989 provided me with a disaster. It began with a brilliant hot day in Rockport, a most attractive town of various coloured houses hung with flower baskets and window boxes. It was one of those blue, white and gold days with children, flinging spray, in and out of the sea; the white sails of yachts passing leisurely by, while speed-boats ploughed foam-furrows through the water.

By now an arthritic hip prevented me from more activity than finding a comfortable place on the sand. Later that evening, after a happy family supper and mellowed with wine, I was cajoled by the children into story-telling. It was half-past nine and I could think of nothing but sinking into a chair with a book. But first, I must pull down my bedroom blind for which purpose I jumped on my bed under the window and stretched up to reach the blind.

With loose sandals I was standing on a slippery quilt, and an extra stretch up was fatal. I fell with a loud thump, flat on my back on a hard floor. That moment is with me yet – the pain, the awareness that I'd done something bad. Catherine and Derek drove me to the health care centre at which an X-ray revealed a splintered fifth vertebra. "It'll be more painful and troublesome than a break," the doctor warned me. And he told Catherine: "Your mother has a considerable degree of arthritis in her spine. I'm surprised she hasn't complained of pain before now."

Since then, I've never been free of pain. Not only arthritis, but osteoporosis played havoc. The damaged fifth vertebra collapsed on to the fourth, and my GP called to say "I'm afraid we can't do anything for you – you're crumbling!" At the time I laughed but have since realised it was anything but funny.

Writing now, in the summer of 1993, I can't stand or walk without support. Two sticks in the house and garden, but for anything longer I have a 'walker' which, on smooth surfaces enables me to walk, at normal pace, anything up to a mile. In fact, my 'trolley' as I call it, is a godsend, the light of my life which enables me to have reasonable outings. I lift it into the car boot and drive to some paved road – in the town, beside a lake or, best of all, on a promenade by the sea.

I've tried physiotherapy, osteopathy, massage, acupuncture, and spiritual healing. None have made any difference. The only relief I get is from drugs which, obviously, have disadvantages. One thing this has taught me – the ability, up to a point, not only to put up with pain, but to accept it. Also one must try, as far as possible, not to talk about it. People are kind and prepared to listen so far, but the pain of others is not only unimaginable, but boring. And perhaps the company of others is the best antidote of all. When friends say, "You sound so cheerful," I feel I've won a minor battle.

Meanwhile, reverting to that summer of 1989, eight days after my accident, and a week before flying home, came the day we'd arranged to drive to Amherst and the home of Emily Dickinson.[96] It dawned hot and sunny, and, in face of my doubts, Catherine was keen to take me. It was an eighty-mile

[96] Emily Elizabeth Dickinson, American poet, 1830-1886.

drive along the highway, and we arrived in a blaze of heat. With difficulty I managed to hobble to the main bookshop, and bought several books of Emily's poems and a biography.

Amherst is a pleasant town, rather like those of Northern France, more continental than American. After lunch in a vegetarian restaurant, we drove to 'her' house to find that it wasn't, on that particular day, open to the public. All the same, we walked around it and sat in her beloved garden, now burgeoning with irises, roses, stocks, lilies, thyme and cushiony rock plants.

I felt strongly the spirit of herself and her poetry, perhaps even more so than on last year's visit when we were shown over her house by a guide who didn't capture the essence of herself. She appeared not to know anything of Emily's unrequited love for the Rev. Charles Wadsworth, a fine preacher with strong Calvinist leanings, possessed of intellectual and spiritual magnetism.

Emily seems to have conceived a hopeless passion for him after hearing him preach, though she realised that nothing could come of it with a man happily married and forty years old. At this time, 1854, she herself was twenty-four. Though they wrote to each other, none of their letters survive; and he certainly called on her once. Aware of her plainness, it is probable that these lines apply to that meeting:[97]

> *I take a flower – as I go –*
> *My face to justify*

At that period Massachusetts was swept up in a religious revival springing from a Puritan background.[98] All the members of Emily's family were converted, and most of her friends. It is remarkable that Emily resisted – especially when Wadsworth was a devout exponent.

[97] Extract from *Again His Voice is at the Door*, by Emily Dickinson, first published in 1945.
[98] Great Awakening, reaction against rational Christianity.

Other fragments of her poems came to mind that day as I sat in the garden:

> *Split the lark – and you'll find the music –*
> *Bulb after bulb, in silver rolled –* [99]

and, amid her despair,

> *It was not Death, for I stood up*
> *And all the Dead, lie down –* [100]

Probably it was this that started her custom of always wearing white – as if she were a bride in waiting for him who never came.

One critic observed that although her poems began in bursts of genius, she could not sustain them; certainly they needed trimming and tailoring, but she wrote as she felt and not to please publishers. A true original and startlingly modern for her time, her writing owed much to her wide reading, following a first-class education at Amherst Academy. At any rate, she did to language what no one had ever done before, by using words in a new way. There is something sad about this Lady in White, passionate, yet unfulfilled, who, after a socially active youth, became almost a total recluse before she died at the age of fifty-six.

No doubt I was influenced by Emily Dickinson – her fresh use of words revitalised the language; she created images, sparkling and new. To me, bred on the Victorian Romantics, these poems were a tonic antidote to worn-out forms and expressions. Maybe she lacked form and order; her talent lay in new births of magical oddity:

[99] Extract from *Split the Lark and You'll Find the Music*, by Emily Dickinson, first published in 1896.
[100] Extract from *It Was Not Death for I Stood Up*, by Emily Dickinson, first published in 1891.

I'm nobody,
Who are you?
Are you nobody too?
Then there's a pair of us – don't tell!
They'd banish us, you know!

How dreary to be somebody!
How public like a frog
To tell one's name the livelong day
To an admiring bog! [101]

Here is my own poem on Emily Dickinson:[102]

Others wore colours; I wore white
for one who never came –
whose coming was his going that
left me here alone.
I'll not expect a knocking on
my name carved in stone.

I admire her for her independent spirit, firstly in writing as she felt, never pandering to editors, or being enslaved by rules of grammar, and secondly for swimming alone in her group of friends and relations against the tidal wave of religious revivalism which swept across the country.

---

[101] 'I'm Nobody! Who Are You?' first published in 1891.
[102] 'Emily Dickinson' from *Netting The Sun*, published by Enitharmon, 1989.

Chapter 24

New England Experiences (II)

Already it is August 1993. I'll turn back to May amid doubts as to whether I could make a sixth trip to America. But I left on May 27th and it turned out to be one of the best trips of all. How wonderful it was to arrive in a period of warm sun to see the two little girls aged 6 and 7 at the lovely age of wonder and delight in all that life has to offer.

Catherine, who looked worn and thin after a gruelling course in Biochemistry, made heroic efforts to relax into the holiday spirit. Before long she returned to her true self and we were driving to Concord, Boston and up to Maine.

Although I look back on my days in the States as bathed in bright sunlight, there were interludes of heavy rain falling in steady grey rods. Such was one whole day of a weekend in Ogunquit, Maine. Although we stayed at the luxurious Cliff House Hotel surrounded by every comfort, the 'rain down-poured' and a chill wind blew. To add to our discomfort, Catherine, recovering from a virus infection, coughed the night through. The next day we drove along the coast toward Kennebunkport for a glimpse of the Bush holiday home situated on a projecting arm of the bay. We might have been in the north of England on a misty grey November day.

Perhaps this was the only excursion which wasn't a total success. All the same it ended well and the sun appeared on our last day. After drifting in and out of the gift shops in the romantic Perkin's Cove, I pushed my trolley with Catherine's help, up the rocky headlands with wild white-maned sea horses rearing and plunging below. Here the great unfenced Atlantic Ocean spread out below us on its heaving 3,000 miles to Great Britain. Nearby tiny sea-honeysuckle, rock roses, and bladder campion sprang among the rocks.

Overwhelmed by magnificence, I paused at a bend in the path to look out to sea. A sudden yell from Catherine startled me: my trolley had started its own journey down the rocks. In a split second she leapt forward and saved it. Otherwise without support, I could never have walked back.

A happy interlude between excursions was a poetry reading that Catherine arranged for me in the garden of the Andover bookshop. It was a hot sunny afternoon, and the audience was interested and responsive. Members of the Writer's Group asked questions which led to helpful discussion and better still, from my publisher's viewpoint, many sales. Alas my collected poems *Netting The Sun* had already sold out, so they had to make do with an earlier selection *The Eighth Day* and my 'sworn to be last' volume *Sundowner*. Surprisingly, there is still what must be a final collection *The Leave Train*.

Though reduced to walking and standing with two sticks or a trolley, poems mysteriously arrive as it were, by a side door. They seem to happen when I'm not thinking. But that is in the first exuberant state of creation. Thinking comes with composition, even more with revision, although it can happen that revision ruins a poem making it self-conscious, too clever and deliberate. What I call 'the midnight oil' sort of poem. There is much truth in Keats: "If a poem come not naturally as the leaves to a tree, it had best not come at all."[103] As to prose,

[103] John Keats, British poet, 1795-1821.

I think George Moore had the last word: "A man doesn't write so well once he's learned how to write."[104] Too much concern for form and style stifles spontaneity. Emily Dickinson is a prime example of writing her poems hot from the forge of feeling and imagination – letting syntax and punctuation take care of themselves.

It is remarkable how many poets and philosophers come from Massachusetts still under the influence of the early Pilgrim Fathers, so different from those who come from the Western and Southern States. Though Boston may have the most crime-ridden Chinatown, it has Harvard and the Boston Symphony Orchestra with their remarkable summer performances at Tanglewood in a beautiful pastoral area to the west of the state, a sort of Elysian clearing in an endless forest.

As so often happens, it was chance that led us to the most interesting excursion of all. One of the Writer's Group at my poetry reading advised Catherine; "You must take your mother to the Sleepy Hollow Cemetery in Concord." So we went on a day of burning heat and high humidity during the last week of my holiday.

Unlike any cemetery I've ever seen, this one was a sleepy hollow – at least the lower part was a green basin circled by a narrow sandy road and pleasantly shaded by pine and deciduous trees. The gravestones, grey and low, no marble monstrosities, seemed a natural part of the scene. But our interest was the Writer's Ridge which rose steeply and rockily from the hollow. Doubts as to whether I could manage the steep stony path were settled by Catherine who hauled the trolley before me.

Harried by mosquitoes, we sat on the bank facing the Thoreau family stone inscribed in large letters topping wife and family with the name John, father of Henry David and two girls. Little could they have known how, in the years ahead, the

[104] George Augustus Moore, Irish novelist, short story writer, poet, 1852-1933.

son would overtop the father. Here, while waving off the mosquitoes, we munched our sandwiches and took photographs. A much smaller stone to the left bore one name only – Louisa May Alcott. We wondered where other talented family members lay hidden. But Louisa was the only writer. Climbing further up the path we came to a huge rough-cut rock whose metal plate bore the names of Ralph Waldo Emerson and his wife Lydian, so spelled, though several accounts put her down as Lydia.

Within this circle were many American writers including the novelist Helen Hunt Jackson, best selling novelist friend of Emily Dickinson, and Nathaniel Hawthorne remembered chiefly by his novel *The Scarlet Letter*. One fact impressed me as different from a British graveyard; I exclaimed to Catherine "No crosses!" In fact this particular group were mostly Unitarians. Though Unitarians believe in the historical Jesus as a great prophet, they don't accept him as the one and only Son of God, and obviously not in the Trinity and the Christian creed.

As I mentioned in a previous chapter, from the mid to late eighteenth century the great religious revival in Massachusetts swept up in two great waves, some adhering even more fervently to the literal truth of the New Testament while others backed away. This, to a large extent, is happening in Britain today. Unitarians, like Quakers, are free to choose whatever they believe to be the truth. This elicited a United Reform Church Minister's description of their religion as 'rather shapeless.'

From my own experience of a Unitarian service, and many talks with Quakers, I tend to regard both as sects or cults rather than forms of religion. I attended a Unitarian service with Catherine in Massachusetts. When she queried me afterwards, I said I felt a lack of wonder and awe. Indeed I felt I'd been in a lecture hall rather than a church. All the same, it is up to the

189

adherents to make of it what they will. Undoubtedly the teaching and inclusion of all religions is a step beyond the confines of Orthodox Christian creeds. It is significant that so many poets and philosophers have taken this step, apart from scientists and free-thinkers in all fields.

I remember a day, years ago, when my sister and I touched on this subject. After trying to explain my beliefs and the likelihood of truth expressed in the New Testament, she cut short my faltering pronouncements with: "I've grown out of orthodox religion." Younger, wiser, and more perceptive than me, she was in her own way, more religious.

For me, a religious person is one who has not lost the child's sense of wonder but still sees as Keats said: "everything sparkling and new as on the first day of creation." And also that sense of awe which overwhelms one's own insignificant self – as when one stands on the peak of a mountain range or enters a cathedral with the choir singing and sunlight slanting from the east window.

But I digress from the Sleepy Hollow cemetery. Seldom have I left a graveyard with such a feeling of peace and uplift; of all our excursions I think this is the most potent and I long to return to Massachusetts next year.

Chapter 25

Reflections and Recollections

The calendar has turned to September 1993. The fortune-teller who promised me a ripe old age – until 84 years – may possibly have underestimated my life span, although there are still four months until my 85th birthday. This begs the question, "Do I really want to go on?" On grey days when I see no one, and my arthritic back makes every movement painful, the answer is "No!" But on such as today, with brilliant sun and every garden bursting with colour, and my arthritis is much better, the answer is "Yes!"

It is so important in old age to keep fit mentally as well as physically. On such a day as this I've walked with my trolley beside Anglezarke Reservoir. Today I might have been in the Lake District with sparkling water, grebes diving, willows and reeds rustling along the water's edge. The quarries, long disused, look like natural rock faces, golden brown in the sun, covered with great mats of faded heather. As I sat reflecting on this scene, several people spoke to me in passing. One man got out of his car to ask: "Are you all right? Do you need a lift home?" Another asked if I'd seen a Jack Russell terrier, lost property of a 90 year old man. Then two women chatted about the beauty of the day and the pleasure of walking in such lovely surroundings.

If I'm feeling lonely and have no visitors I put my trolley in the car, drive to some attractive place and walk. I hope that I never see the day when I can neither drive nor walk. On this wonderful day, YES I want to go on living.

Life is all contradictions and challenges. The evening after this perfect day my invaluable gardener/handyman rang to say that he had fallen downstairs, broken several bones and would be off work for weeks. The following day I had a batch of poems returned for the first time, from a magazine that normally published my work. Then I was informed by the Home Help department that cooking services could not be provided unless I was literally on the point of starvation. Since I cannot stand without support, kitchen work is almost impossible. I thanked God for private and paid services.

It is now December 1993, cold and wet after a spell of hard dry frost. My publisher Enitharmon, has accepted another volume of my poems aptly titled *The Leave Train, New and Selected Poems*. Better still, I've been asked to extend this volume to include additional poems from past publications. This has given me a considerable amount of work. In addition to this, I've been asked to co-operate in a biography of my old poet/mentor, Herbert Palmer, by writing the foreword and providing information. So although I've neglected these memoirs for several months, my time has been wholly taken up.

Inevitably, at this time of year, one's thoughts and shopping lists are turned toward Christmas. Everyone complains of the rush, the commercialism, and the worry of it all. Yet we continue to exchange card for card and present for present. So good will merges with competition. As usual, I dread the onslaught of the festive season, especially difficult when shopping must be undertaken with my trolley.

Christmas has now passed with half the population struck by a debilitating virus to which I succumbed. Despite my poor state of health, my son Martin graciously brought me, complete with trolley, walking sticks and medicines, to their home on Christmas Eve. During dinner that evening, I heard the good news that my third great grandchild was expected in 1994! "Will I still be alive by then?" I asked myself. A pertinent question because now it is the third week in January 1994 with my 85th birthday at the end of the month. My doctor announced cheerfully: "Your heart, lungs, everything is in splendid working order. You'll live to be a hundred!"

Old age! Most people in their mid-eighties say, "It's not much fun getting old." Two of my contemporaries live in 'Homes for the Living Dead'. This is not their choice but, due to chronic illness, they are physically unable to look after themselves. How fortunate I am to walk with my trolley on smooth paths, even though my longing to tramp over the moors and hills cannot be fulfilled. I have excellent sight and hearing and am able to drive locally. Not only can I still write, I'm running a writers group and have a new volume of poems to be published later this year. It seems gross ingratitude to complain about anything.

It is early February 1994 and a huge bouquet of flowers has arrived from my publisher to congratulate me on the upcoming publication of a collection of poems. "Will I still be alive by autumn of this year?" I asked myself. I had already celebrated my 85th birthday on January 29th with a party given by Martin and Jutta who provided the most splendid food and wine. It was altogether a truly memorable occasion. In his birthday speech, Martin emphasised that the fortune-teller had been mistaken by predicting that I'd live to 84 years!

During the following weeks, I took part in a 30 minute BBC radio programme *Write Now* which was broadcast on four North West channels. To my surprise I was asked to speak for the entire half hour. Usually each speaker is allotted five minutes only. Whether this honour compensates for the fact of

j

being 85, is doubtful. Old age, it seems, brings some rewards for hard work.

I had several visits from Vernon Sproxton, a United Reform church minister with whom I had become a close friend.[105] He worked for many years with the BBC, arranging religious broadcasts for television and radio. He had an amazing flair for this work, combining practical and technical skills with imagination. Although his subjects were theology and philosophy, he loved and understood poetry and music. From the 1950s onwards he gave me work in his programmes and included one or two of my poems in radio broadcasts.

Over the years I'd talked at length with people whose lives were concerned with vital subjects – life, art, love, death and the ever-recurring question: "What, if anything, comes next?" One evening I asked my friend Vernon how, in the face of universal suffering, and the personal ills and distresses of old age, he could believe in ultimate purpose. He was fascinated by the idea of time – a series of events which are subsequent on only one level of consciousness and which are circular rather than linear and can be played back and foreseen as in dreams or intuitive flashes. We talked about our experiences of dreams of future events. Other people have experienced dreams from the past which become vivid in the present.

Many people have experienced the inexplicable, too many to deny possible survival of our 'real' selves. Consolation lies for me in the fact that however searching our questions, we cannot know the answers. The worst thing of all would be to know, to have no need to ask, no capacity for wonder. And wonder surely, is the foundation of all enquiry, scientific discovery is the essence of art and delight. We continue to ask two questions about life: "Why was there ever anything at all?" and "What next?" Though knowing there are no answers, it is the search that keeps us alive.

[105] Vernon Sproxton, religious broadcaster and theologian, 1920-1996.

194

Chapter 26

Summing Up

It is May 16th 1994, a damp grey, near-winter day and I find it difficult to end this memoir. Like life itself, there is always something more.

I clearly recall the month of February which is often referred to as 'the snow month'. This year the snow descended on the north of England in a raging blizzard which blew all night. The following morning I opened the kitchen door to be confronted by walls of snow in the garage.

Forgetting my crumbling spine, I picked up a brush and cleared a path into the garage. I brushed the snow from the surfaces lest it should melt and resolve itself into a flood. The next day I could hardly move, not from mere stiffness, but from severe back pain. After a few weeks I was admitted to the local hospital and found myself among 28 patients in the Orthopaedic ward. One woman with her leg in plaster yelled "Take my leg out nurse! Take my leg out." I put up with this for an hour then, exasperated beyond bearing, I shouted to a passing nurse: "For God's sake, cut it off!" The patient was moved to a side ward.

It appeared that I had a wedge fracture for which time and patience were the only remedies. I was moved to a nursing home situated in attractive countryside. The day room looked over a lake fringed by large forest trees in which squirrels performed acrobatics, coming to rest as they raised question mark tails. Their performance seemed to fit perfectly in this atmosphere of disturbed patients. One of my poems *From the Day Room* begins: [106]

The people here are not here.
Where are they gone who have left themselves behind?

After four days of unrest I moved back home, but finding myself unable to manage, I went to Croston Park – a lovely white eighteenth century rectory, converted into a Rest Home. Jane Austen might well have lived here where two spacious rooms look out through three circular bay windows on to the garden – a miracle of crocuses and daffodils in the spring – with lush meadows and huge beech and oak trees. Few inmates seemed to appreciate the beauties of nature, and were more concerned with their own bodily comforts.

Unlike my previous nursing home experience, there were no depressing circles of armchairs facing the television or an empty fireplace. Each person had their own special chair and woe unto anyone who tried to annexe it. Strange quirks were a feature of several women residents, one of whom carried a cushion from which she refused to be parted. Another, autocratic and bossy, insisted on her favourite TV programmes, switching off the choices of others. But most people were quiet and reasonable.

It is now August 1994. My proposed visit to the States in June was frowned upon by several people who thought I was unfit to travel. But despite their protestations, I left for Boston on June 3rd. From the moment of being met by Catherine and the two little girls, this turned out to be a most spectacular

---

[106] Extract from a poem in *The Leave Train*, published by Enitharmon, 1994.

visit. To begin with, I left rain and a temperature of 54 degrees in Manchester and arrived in Boston to a lovely warm 77 degrees. I felt transformed into another person.

Although a year older than last year, which I'd vowed would be my final adventure, I managed to do almost as much as on previous visits. This was in spite of Catherine's full programme: driving the girls to soccer matches, swimming and piano lessons, and birthday parties. Not to mention the endless shopping, household chores and gardening.

On this visit we had an epic day at Henry Longfellow's home in Cambridge. To begin with, the whole area sweltered under an untimely 'Bermuda High' with the thermometer climbing to 96 degrees.[107] Together with the humidity, the heat seemed almost unbearable.

For Catherine it was a rare free day. Lying on the bed that morning I swore, "I can't make that trip." But Catherine had the car ready and waiting at the front door. We parked in the outskirts of the city and negotiated two underground stations to Harvard Square. Valiantly she pulled my trolley up numerous flights of stairs. Never since my back injury had I climbed so many steps. Emerging from the underground onto Brattle Street, we were met by blasts of hot air and walked – happily underneath the trees – to the Longfellow House.

I was overwhelmed by this experience which, at home, I would never have undertaken. Under the bright blue sky we admired the large Georgian house painted a primrose shade of yellow. Having arrived well before the house opened, we retreated to the merciful shade of the garden and gazed at the sundial as George Washington had done when he used the house as his headquarters during the siege of Boston.

Inside the house and under the direction of an excellent guide, we climbed the long steep staircase into the poet's

[107] A subtropical area of high pressure in the North Atlantic Ocean off the East Coast of North America.

living quarters – assembled as they had been in his lifetime. The dining room table was set with an opened bottle of wine and glasses as it was on the night he entertained Dickens and other literary celebrities. Longfellow gave many such parties; he particularly enjoyed the company of English poets.

A good conversationalist, he gave many lectures. Teaching was his vocation – having had positions at Bowdoin in Maine and later at Harvard before he discovered himself as a poet.

He adored his three daughters; several paintings are witness to this as are these lines from *The Children's Hour*.[108]

> *From my study I see in the lamplight,*
> *Descending the broad hall stair*
> *Grave Alice, and laughing Allegra,*
> *And Edith with golden hair.*

The mental picture I most clearly remember is of his beloved wife Fanny who was burned to death when her billowing dress caught fire. She shrieked in terror and Henry rushed to her aid. He badly burned his own hands and face in a vain effort to save her.

Overwhelmed by grief, he couldn't eat, sleep or write. Much later something of his feelings surfaced in the '*Cross of Snow*':[109]

> *In the long, sleepless watches of the night,*
> *A gentle face – the face of one long dead –*
> *Looks at me from the wall, where round its head*
> *The night-lamp casts a halo of pale light.*

Unlike much modern poetry, Longfellow's poems have a way of clinging to the brain. Back home I couldn't find a single Longfellow poem in my many anthologies. Due to inevitable

---

[108] Extract from 'The Children's Hour', first published in 1863.
[109] Extract from 'Cross of Snow' written in 1879, lately published in *Selected Poems*, Penguin, 1988.

changes in poetic style, he suffered the same fall in popularity as did Tennyson. Nevertheless he had become the most popular American poet of his day.

A true Victorian, Longfellow was an orderly man, conventional, courteous. Above all he was respectable. Something of his character is reflected in his verse. Yet this cursory summary by no means gives you a picture of the whole man. Deep feelings were masked by his strict upbringing. He suffered from black depressions and periods of gloom, nursing grief and disappointment. He never fully recovered from his wife Fanny's death and was painfully conscious of falling short of his ideals. Lines from his poem *Mezzo Cammin* illustrate these feelings:[110]

> *Half my life is gone and I have let*
> *The years slip from me and have not fulfilled*
> *The aspiration of my youth, to build*

Thoughtful and kind, Longfellow lionised, yet always human, was a 'nice' man. Somehow I think he sounds rather dull.

A separate visit to his favourite Wayside Inn at Sudbury seems to contradict this impression. Built in 1716, it is supposedly the oldest inn in America. Longfellow and his friends spent many evenings by the fire, drinking the hours away. Thus *Tales of A Wayside Inn*, one of his best-known poems, was born.[111] I doubt whether his group would have enjoyed the exotic meal offered to Catherine and me which, alas, we were unable to eat. We settled for a salad which was enormous and prevented us from tackling their famous Baked Indian pudding. We were cheered, on this blazing hot day, to be offered a glass of good English beer. Much of the inn was

[110] Extract from *Mezzo Cammin* written in 1842, published in *Life of Henry Wadsworth Longfellow,* 1866.

[111] *Tales of a Wayside Inn,* first published by Boston, Ticknor and Fields, 1863.

preserved as originally built as shown by the old oak beams and uneven wooden floors. Despite our longing to linger in the colourful garden, we drove back at speed, in time to meet the school bus which faithfully brought the little girls safely home each day.

Not one of these adventures would have been possible without Catherine's help, driving, supporting me with my trolley up stairs, steps and banks. Here in black and white I can tell her what these visits meant to me.

I constantly recall the wonderful life and fulfilling relationships I've had. Such reflections inevitably lead to the evergreen question: "What is it all about?" I believe that no one can live happily without a sense of purpose. While some believe in divine purpose, I ask myself: "Is there any other purpose in life beyond that which we put into it?"

We're thrown back on mystery and my personal creed: "I love the mystery that has no name." One of the mysteries is that when you think all is finished and you've come to the end of the road, other paths open up. This brings to mind a poem of mine:[112]

What Is God?

I have not seen God face to face –
how can I love him
whose answers to my questions are
silences in stone and star,
whose presence is my loneliness?

Incomprehensible Three-in-One,
how can I love thee
One-in-Three?

[112] 'What Is God?' from *The Eighth Day*, published by Enitharmon, 1980.

I love ordinary people
touchable, fallible
speaking my own tongue.

I love the real sun
whose warmth I feel
in whose light I live.
I love the green sap rising
from darkness into apple,
ape and man
becoming breath, mind, spirit –
invisible, intangible
three in one.
I love the mystery
that has no name.

On that note, it is time to bring the journey through my long and colourful life to a close.

Conclusion
by Catherine Robinson

The journey through my mother Phoebe's life has been an incredibly enriching experience. She wrote exactly as she felt and although readers may have found the time line a little tricky to follow, it is the nature of her writing. I have compiled and edited the memoir but the essential core of her story is unchanged.

Her creative talent revealed itself during early days at boarding school. As she recalls in an earlier chapter "Words became a fascination, leaping into scansion and rhyme, making patterns and colours." Among her personal writings, letters and diaries, I found snippets of early verse, evidence of her budding talent which blossomed over the years. At the end of her schooling she was tempted to apply to Oxford University but the need for freedom was a much stronger force. Her return home was a turning point after which she was able to write freely, far away from the demands of the academic world.

She openly acknowledged the influence, strength and power of personal relationships upon her writing which was most prolific from the late 1940s until the 1980s. During these years she experienced the greatest heights of sadness and joy, including the deaths of her son and husband and the birth of her daughter. We can speculate that these events and the influence of her family, friends and mentors were fundamental to the profound depth of her writing.

Our move to Ireland in 1978 marked another turning point in her life after which she travelled to see us once or twice each year. She revelled in the beauty of the countryside while enjoying our home. When the news came of my family's pending move to the USA she was devastated and wrote in an earlier chapter "I put down the telephone and wept." However, she continued to visit and opened doors into the literary world of New England. After each of her visits to the USA, she would say laughingly, "This is my last visit. I shan't be here next year!" Happily, the next year would see her flying over to see us.

In fact she made a total of eight trips across the Atlantic. Energetic and lively, Phoebe kept us on our toes and each day we were on the move to new and exciting places. She came to our girls' soccer games, gave poetry readings at our local bookstore and elementary schools and a broadcast for local cable television. This was in addition to trips to local seaside towns and her many literary 'pilgrimages'. She delighted in simple pleasures such as walking around our neighbourhood in Andover, Massachusetts. She relished the visits to our local ice cream parlour where we would sit outside sucking on vanilla cones topped with chocolate.

Phoebe visited us for the last time in 1998 at the age of 89. We had moved to Arizona and the long transatlantic journey was tough as she had become quite frail. She was determined to make the trip and as always, we enjoyed her entertaining company. After returning home from this visit she suffered an incapacitating stroke with the result that she was unable to take care of herself. Besides, living alone in her bungalow had become difficult with her advancing age and physical frailty.

My brother Martin and his wife Jutta took charge of the sale of her house and the move to a nursing home. It was a very hard time for everyone but despite her protests, Phoebe knew that this was an inevitable move.

Phoebe was well looked after during her seven year stay. True to form, she kept the staff on their toes. She also kept the residents amused and entertained. One evening when the staff was extremely busy, Phoebe was assisted to the bathroom. After some time had passed, she became impatient and used her cell phone to call 999, the emergency services number. An officer duly appeared at the front door and said, "I believe one of your residents needs attention." This resulted in much laughter and we joked about the incident on many occasions afterwards.

Phoebe died in February 2005 at the age of 96. Always thinking ahead, she had planned her funeral service and cremation many years prior to her death. She had chosen the hymns and prayers and carefully mapped out the order of the service. As for the reception afterwards, she had said: "I want everyone to enjoy themselves knowing that I have moved to a much better place." Thus we raised our glasses to her with Veuve Clicquot, her favourite champagne.

Phoebe asked that we, her family, spread her ashes on her beloved moorland. We carried out her request on Anglezarke Moor – close to her old home – while reciting her poem *A Box Of Silver Birch*.[113] Toward the end of our small ceremony, a skylark circled above us and sang as if to send her on her way.

> *Give me a box of silver birch,*
> *something light and easily burnt,*
> *but don't enclose me*
> *airless in earth; I belong to the moors*
> *the miles of bracken and heather.*
> *I've been a prisoner long enough*
> *now let me be wherever*
> *the changing wind blows me.*

[113] Published in *A Box Of Silver Birch* by Enitharmon, 1997.